HOW I FORCED PANDORA'S BOX SHUT

BY SAMANTHA WHITE

ISBN 978-1-5272-9821-7 (Paperback)
ISBN 978-1-3999-0179-6 (eBook)

Edited by Katharine Beaton
Book production by Dawn James, Publish and Promote
Cover design by Publish and Promote
Interior design and layout by Perseus Design

Printed and bound in the United Kingdom.

Note to the reader:
The events in this book are based on the author's memories from her perspective. Certain names have been changed to protect the identities of those mentioned. Any similarity to real persons, places, incidents, or actions is coincidental. The information is provided for educational purposes only. In the event you use any of the information in this book for yourself, which is your constitutional right, the author and publisher assume no responsibility for your actions.

CONTENTS

CHAPTER 1

DOWNFALL

January 12, 2021

After watching three episodes of *Released*—an OWN special on YouTube, I could not watch anymore. These episodes depicted the struggles of ex-offenders while being reintroduced into society. What touched me about this program was that it showed how their families were impacted by them being incarcerated, among other things. Seeing how their relatives had initially been impacted, and were still being impacted by their incarceration, snatched me back to my sixteen-year-old self when I had my entire life turned upside down upon receiving one phone call.

It was a lovely Sunday afternoon, the last Sunday of August in 2004. I was effortlessly laying on a nude and red striped sofa in the living room, relaxing and gazing indifferently at the thirty-four-inch black television that was positioned in the middle of the Victorian window frames. I was in a trance-like state as I was elated about commencing my A Levels at Kingston College, United Kingdom, that upcoming Wednesday—the first of September. The ringing of my mobile phone pulled me back to reality. Nonchalantly, I picked my phone up; it was my mother. With no care in the world, I answered.

"Hello mom, what's up?" I said casually.

"Nardia, they arrested me," she said candidly. Nardia is my nickname, which was given to me by my mother.

My eyes widened, and I jumped up to a seating position on the sofa. "What?! What do you mean!?" I said as my chest started to tighten.

"I'm in Bristol police station. They gave me a phone call to ring you," she said bluntly.

My mother had gone to Bristol last night with her boyfriend. Earlier in the day, she had decided not to go, but then later, her boyfriend—a native Bristolian—persuaded her to go with him. In fact, there was a party being held somewhere in South London and she was supposed to attend, but she changed her mind at the last minute. As I was going to be on my own and I had nothing else planned, she persuaded me to visit my grandmother's friend, Joan, who resided down the road from us in Clapham South in South West London.

Panic-stricken, my voice cracked as I said, "What is going to happen to me!?"

It was a question that had no resolution in my mind. This question set me on a tangent of worry. I was frozen, numb, and shocked, weighed down by the flood of questions. How was I going to cope? Where was I going to live? How was I going to live? Who was going to take care of me? A reservoir of questions came rushing down, shattering my well-planned wall of ideology into a pile of broken pieces.

A second ago, I had all my ducks in a row. I was going to start my A Levels: Biology, Chemistry, Mathematics, and Physics. I was going to be the first person in my family to attend university. I was going to be a doctor—possibly a surgeon—Dr. White. In July of this year, I achieved a milestone that my mother had never done; I graduated secondary school with ten GCSEs with approximately 15 months education in the UK. My life, or the life that I had hoped for, flashed in front of my eyes. The light of hope just flickered out. A piece of my soul died with this revelation from my mother.

"Nardia, Nardia, are you there?" called my mother.

The sound ripped me back to reality.

"Yes," I said reluctantly. "What's going to happen to me? What should I do?"

She told me to contact her sponsor, Angela Dove. I noted down her address and confirmed that I would visit her home next Saturday.

"What happens now?" I asked confused, coupled with a sound of fear in my voice.

"They are going to process me and then I think I'll be speaking to a solicitor, and I think I'm going to jail after," she said.

That entire conversation, all those statements, were a blur as I kept drifting in and out of it. I felt as though I was being submerged underwater. Everything was a blur. The phone call ended. I shouted to Joan, my grandmother's friend, who was in the kitchen preparing Sunday dinner. Joan ran into the living room.

"What happened?" she said with confusion.

"My mom just rang me and told me that she was arrested last night. Apparently, she was caught up in a stakeout. Marlon, her boyfriend, was on Bristol's wanted list. I believe for domestic violence towards his child's mother, pushing dope—purchasing and supplying, and some other charges. They found drugs in the house where they were residing, and she stayed loyal to him: the prisoner's dilemma."

The rest of the day remained a blur. I was going through the motions, but I was numb. I felt trapped in an emotional fortress suspended in thin air. Not one person could reach me. Joan tried her best to console me, but it was to no avail. I felt trapped and unreachable. An *Alice in Wonderland* moment. The more I learnt, the further down the rabbit hole I was dragged. It all happened so quickly. I could not get a foothold on the situation, and it was all out of my control. I saw my aspirations, dreams and hopes being buried right in front of my eyes.

I did not know what to do. I was experiencing the brunt of other people's decisions—mainly my mother's—and I was thrown into this mess with no fault of my own. Searching my heart, mind, and soul for a solution or some semblance of normalcy gave me a migraine. Finding the solution to this problem appeared to be beyond my mental capacity.

I was emotionally and physically drained from trying to devise a plan or strategy to overcome this situation. I could not decipher a way out of this darkness and now I was exhausted and overwhelmed. Discouraged, I went home to retrieve some clothes to start college in a few days and for the forseeable uncertain future.

Tuesday night arrived, 31st of August, and I struggled to sleep. The elation that I had been floating upon earlier that day felt like a world away.

Disjointed Dream
***

That night, I dreamt that I was back in school in Jamaica. DeCarteret College (DC) was the name of my secondary school.

I had just learned that I made it into my school's debating team to represent them on School Challenge Quiz which was a lifelong dream of mine. During the weeks approaching the event, I worked extremely hard with my team members, teachers, and coaches.

School was my everything in Jamaica. I was extremely active, committing to as many societies as were afforded to me: Girl Guides, Red Cross, Dance Society, the Net Ball team, and now the Debating Society.

For this big event, we were measured for special blazers which were dark purple with DC's logo on the left breast. Standing at five foot four, I oscillated between an extra small and a small, and on this occasion, I was delegated a small. This was because I had to wear the blazer in collaboration with my uniform—a crispy white plain t-shirt and a plain black skirt made from the same material as the blazer that sat just below my knee (school's policy), combined with equally crispy white plain socks folded immaculately above my ankle and paired with sensible jet-black shoes.

I admired myself proudly in the mirror, as I looked at how well my blazer fitted my frame. I whispered to myself, "Well done, girl. You made the team." I was beaming.

The event organiser called our team—it was time. We approached the panel in the order designed and agreed on by our teachers and coaches. My specialism was Geography and Mathematics. We were neck and neck with our competitors.

In the final round, the invigilator asked, "Where is the start of the global timing system?"

I tapped the buzzer. I emphatically answered, "Bristol, United Kingdom."

He denounced my answer—I was wrong.

The other team said, "Greenwich, London, UK."

I was shocked because I knew that answer. I was simply not as specific as the other team, by including the actual location Greenwich. The need for time—hence the global timing system—was due to the train journeys that took place between London and Bristol, and the conductors, among other people, needing to manage their time effectively. The other team exploded with victory. I was gutted! I let my team down, I let my school down too, but most importantly, I let myself down.

The pain that I felt, jolted me back to reality. I jerked back in surprise. Joan was shaking me, trying to wake me up.

***

My first week of college was bittersweet. That entire week I felt like I was just existing. I felt like a rolling moss being moved by the wind and gathering no debris. I started classes but there was no excitement; my emotions were stifled. I did not have a future, all I had was the present. I could not see past the present.

Bright and early Saturday morning, I set off to go to Deptford to visit Angela D, as instructed by my mother. I eagerly approached her door, pressed her buzzer, and looked up towards her window while holding my breath. Nothing.

I rang her buzzer two more times. On the second attempt, I saw a ruffling of her curtains. To draw their attention, I waved with a sense of urgency at the person who was looking at me. With swiftness, they speedily closed the curtains. With complete naivety and vulnerability, I stood at the entrance of her door with the greatest of expectations that someone would open the door and let me into her flat.

Five minutes passed. Nothing! Another five minutes went by with still no change. Numb. I felt as though a piece of my heart was ripped out of my chest. I reluctantly wiped away the salt-filled tears from the corner of my mouth. I felt rejected; I felt alone; I felt lost, and I felt empty. With a deep inhale and exhale, I dropped my head with acceptance and disappointment, and with a ninety degree pivot to my right, I turned and walked away with a promise never to return.

While walking towards the bus stop, a barrage of thoughts consumed my mind: *What more can I expect; who is she to take on my mother's responsibility? She made a promise to my mother, which she has now relinquished. Should I hate her? That is not fair on her. She does not know me. Her not turning up for me does not make my situation any worse.*

What I had learned that past week was that life is filled with nothing but curveballs. One moment, you have the twinkle of excitement in your eyes, and you are overjoyed with expectations, and in the next moment, all your hopes and dreams are pulled like a rug from beneath your feet. I boarded the 177 bus heading towards Peckham as I pondered my thoughts. Once I arrived in Peckham, I disembarked the bus, and got on the 345 heading towards South Kensington.

As Brixton police station approached on the left-hand side of the road, I jerked to attention and pressed the bell. I disembarked the bus and continued left down Brixton Road to the market area. I walked through Brixton market and emerged onto Coldharbour Lane. I took a left and then I continued walking straight until I approached the salon—my mom's friend's designated hairdressing salon where she was renting a chair.

As I entered the salon, Jennifer, my mom's friend, trotted eagerly over to me wide-eyed, asking whether I had the opportunity to speak to Angela. I confirmed that I did not get the chance to speak to her and that someone in her flat had pulled the curtain and peeked through and when they saw that it was me, they had pulled the curtain back.

"What?! How could she do such a harsh thing?!" exclaimed Jennifer.

"That's alright," I said while shrugging my shoulders.

"I did promise your mom that I would do what I could to help. You can come and work for me on

Saturdays—wash and blow-dry hair and braid the base in preparation for me to weave them. You can help around the shop with tidying up, sweeping, and ad hoc activities," reassured Jennifer.

I was overwhelmed. Tears started to stream down my face as I thanked her.

CHAPTER 2

TURMOIL

A fter thirty minutes of frantically rummaging through the cupboard, I was fuming.

"Why do I have to do this?" I mourned.

I had been pulling out bags of rubbish—old carrier bags, crumbled plastic bags, and travel bags—for what felt like hours. It had been a long and tumultuous day. Exhausted from a long day at work, I had to come to the flat where I resided with my mother before her incarceration, to clear and remove my mother's and my stuff. Earlier today, I had purchased and collected two large barrels to store my mother's belongings away and eventually ship them to Jamaica when I could afford to do so.

Having to sort through and clear out this cupboard was frustrating because I was forced to be the adult in this entire situation. I had always been made to be the adult. My mother gave birth to me at sixteen and I felt like that had stunted her progress—her emotional maturity—at that moment in time.

All the rubbish was jam-packed into the cupboard. I stumbled upon an azure plastic bag, meticulously wrapped. It was a little bit larger than my hand and was sitting at the back of the cupboard. Casually, I picked it up. It felt heavy, despite its dimensions. It intrigued me; but not thinking too deeply into it, I placed the bag on the floor along with the other stuff and proceeded to empty the cupboard. This cupboard was positioned at the top of a very steep wooden staircase. It was being shared by my mom and one other housemate in a flat that was in Tulse Hill, South West London. I shared a double room with my mother in a three-bedroom flat. I had been living here for almost two years.

Three Years Earlier
***

Rose (roses) Farquharson was a beautiful woman both inside and out. A praying woman with a heart of gold, she had taught me the meaning of excellence, resiliency, and tenacity. She never accepted half-hearted efforts. She was a tough cookie who taught all her grandchildren lifelong lessons in her own unique way. If any of her, eight grandchildren, at any point, were given chores, we were expected to complete them to perfection. If we fell short at any point—swept the yard haphazardly, for example—we would have to repeat the task and expect her inspection thereafter. Through her harsh lessons, I learned that life needed you to show up and do your best in all areas. Her lessons instilled in us healthy competition; we were always competing amongst each other, especially during exam sessions. Nonetheless, we were each other's cheerleaders.

Four years earlier, I had resided with my mother in a two-bedroom house in Mike Town, Manchester, Jamaica. I had my own room that was fully furnished. It was huge, light, and airy. I was in a bubble that was my atmosphere. The world was my oyster then. I even dreamed of representing Jamaica as Miss Universe or Miss World. I was five foot four at twelve years old going on thirteen years old, so my aspirations were plausible, if I kept growing.

As I was an only child, my mother requested for my older cousin to live with us to keep me company. My room was so big that my cousin was given her own double bed, bedside table, and chest of drawers. With all that furniture jam-packed into my bedroom, one would think that we would be falling over each other, but we did not. Plenty of room remained for us to exercise in front of our beds at our own convenience.

Did I receive any special treatment? No. My cousin and I were treated the same; we were allocated the same number of chores and responsibilities. We had to have each other's backs against my mother and her potential partners. My mother would dress us the same—so much so that people used to ask whether we were fraternal twins because we did not look alike, yet we were the same size and height. We lived a great life. We even had a lady that would come over every weekend to wash our clothes—except our uniforms, that was our responsibility.

Thriving and going about her business, my mother was an extremely brilliant and talented businessperson. She had the Midas touch; every venture that she engaged in was a success. I admired her; she was my hero.

At sixteen years old, after having given birth to me, she had dropped out of high school. I learned that my mother's teachers pleaded with her to return, but she did not. Upon discovering her decision to walk a path less travelled, I was devastated. I mourned her lost opportunities, and her inability to not realise her potential. It was a pathology that raged rampantly throughout my bloodline: no one graduating from school with any qualifications. Despite navigating a path not well-trodden, she was determined to become someone and prove her family and naysayers wrong.

With three businesses under her belt, her next move was to become a homeowner. She had even spoken to the landlord of the house that we lived in about purchasing it if its owner—who resided in the United States—was interested in forgoing their ownership. I beamed with pride. Her life was a blueprint that proved to me that anything is possible with focus, determination, and resilience.

Then she met Sledge Easy. An ugly-spirited man from Kingston who snatched the wind of soaring success from beneath her wings. An energy vampire who left wreckage in his wake. It was the start of a downward spiral, and without forewarning, she admonished all her commitments, dreams, and livelihood to migrate to the United Kingdom. And a year later, with no preparation, I was snatched out of my seconday school - Decarteret College, away from my friends and from my normalcy to a foreign land.

Migrating to the UK was excruciatingly traumatic. I felt out of place. I mourned the loss of my bond with my immediate family and friends, and my life and the normalcy of my routine. I felt like a plant being repotted, but the soil that I was dropped in did not nourish me. My body, mind, and soul were out of alignment. My dreams were snatched from me, and I never recovered. I am still grieving the loss of my aspirations, dreams, and goals.

A Path Least Travelled: July 2002

***

July 20, 2002

Early Saturday morning, I woke up, had a bath, and got ready. Grandma Rose made breakfast as per usual, and we ate. A deep inhalation of crispy fresh country air encapsulated my lungs. I held it there for a few seconds and I repeated this process several times. As the sun peeped over the shoulders of luscious trees, it kissed my cheeks for the last time in Jamaica. The impending journey ignited a pep in my step. Apprehension fuelled me as I knew that this was a new stage in my life; however, I was not sure what it would look like. I took a final look around and made a mental memory, then grabbed my suitcase, and we boarded the mini-bus to Mandeville—Manchester's capital.

Arriving in Mandeville, I spent a couple of hours searching for my father to no avail. To say I was disappointed would be an understatement. My mother purchased my ticket and all she asked my father to do was to give me fifty pounds for pocket money to have while travelling. My grandmother and I asked everyone who knew of him, but he was nowhere to be found. As time progressed, my disappointment transformed into disgruntlement and anger.

"He is such a useless excuse of a man!" I lamented to my nan.

He had been a disappointment my entire life—a perpetual liar who operated through life with the utilisation of avoidance. He would stick his head in the sand, pretending that all was well in the world, while he rolled from one household to the next, leaving a child in his wake.

Due to his inability to be a dependable dad, father, or the man that I required in my time of need, I had to beg my mother's friend, Moodey, to give me the money. I thanked him and informed him that had it not been for him, I would be travelling to an unknown country with no pocket money. Thereafter, I went to say goodbye to my friends, who were also my mother's friends.

Before boarding my transportation to Kingston, I gave my grandmother the longest hug, showered her with love, and promised to stay in contact. My grandmother boarded me onto a bus Kingston-bound where my aunt (her daughter) resided and would be awaiting my arrival.

As the bus moved off in the distance, my eyes filled up with tears. My grandmother had been my saviour; she raised me from a newborn baby to seven years old, when I met my mother, her daughter. My grandmother was my true and only love and I did not know when I would be able to see and hug her again. That thought shattered my final emotional wall. I cried in silence and sniffled for most of my journey to Kingston from Mandeville, Manchester.

Around approximately three hours later, the bus arrived at the Kingston bus garage. While entering the bus terminal, I kept an eager eye out for my Aunt Charmaine, my mother's older and very dependable sister. Disembarking the bus, I saw her across the road, on the pavement adjacent to the bus garage. I greeted her then followed in her direction with my suitcase ensue. She was excited to see me and even more so elated about my journey the following day. I was extremely anxious, but to maintain her level of energy, I simply shook my head to agree with her sentiments and followed her lead.

Upon arriving at her house, I was greeted by her husband and her second son, who was no more than seven years old. In some way, his big bright eyes and his juvenile effervescence put me at ease. I particularly noted that he was years beyond children his age. Aunty Charmaine later informed me that he would read his brother's storybooks. His brother and I were the same age; he was only one week older than me. I was impressed.

July 21, 2002

The next morning arrived. As I had breakfast, I was quite sombre; I had accepted my fate. Due to the location of my aunt's house, I was able to see Kingston's airport (Norman Manley Airport) across the water while sitting on the veranda. I bid farewell to another set of family and my aunt, and I took a cab to the airport. On my way to the airport, it dawned on me that I did not know when I would return, so I wound the left window down with an aim to focus hard on remembering everything that I saw. At that point, I wished that I could capture the sun in a jar to take it with me.

At the airport, my aunt stayed with me until I was assigned a flight attendant and boarded the flight. As I was fourteen years old, I was considered a minor and could not fly on my own. I was among seven other children that were all migrating to different cities across the UK to meet their families (parents/guardians) for holiday or to live there permanently. This was the usual pattern; children would travel to another country on summer holidays, and depending on their family, may remain there for schooling and then eventually become permanent residents.

We were all a huge bundle of nerves and all in the same boat together. It was our first time travelling to the UK and we all had limited knowledge about the country and its demographics. We built comradery in knowing that we were passing through the same right of passage simultaneously, and as such, we huddled together along our journey.

My journey to the United Kingdom seemed like it took ages. It was my first time at the airport as I did not get to see my mother off when she had left the year prior. My flight occurred early in the morning, and I journeyed from Norman Manley Airport to Montego Bay's Sangster

International Airport. All the other children and I were kept together by two flight attendants. We spent all day in Sangster International airport as the second flight was scheduled to leave quite late—around 11:45 p.m.—approximately twelve hours of waiting.

July 22, 2002

Early Monday morning, disembarking from the aeroplane was surreal and chaotic. My focus was to collect my suitcase, and to not lose my invitation letter, which I needed to make available in the presence of an immigration officer—as instructed by my mother. I was placed beside another girl around my age that was on her way to the north of England; I believe it was Birmingham. We were separated at Heathrow upon arrival, and I never spoke to her again.

The atmosphere in the queue through to immigration was buzzing with a sense of fear and uncertainty. Most people's faces were contorted with worry as they were wondering whether they would be detained and sent back. Rumours of several people who smuggled drugs and other illegal paraphernalia and were sentenced to years in jail ran rampant across Jamaica, so the arrival of a flight from the Caribbean, especially Jamaica, resulted in a massive operation. The process was exhaustive and impacted both the passengers and the UK resources. I had to walk past humongous drug-trained dogs. That experience was traumatic. If the dogs sensed that any remnants of drugs lingered on them, people were being pulled out of the queue for further questioning. My mother and several other family members warned me to not trust anyone on the flight—especially to not hold anything for anyone—so I followed their instructions accordingly.

It was my turn to speak to someone at immigration. I gave the Indian lady my passport and invitation letter—this was all we needed in 2002. She asked me about my purpose for visiting; I told her, and I was given a six-month stamp in my passport. I was then ushered out to the entrance where people congregated awaiting the arrival of their families and friends.

As I walked cautiously towards the crowd, I was in awe and overwhelmed as I reflected on my journey. I was excited! I vowed to become someone, to make my grandmother proud. Then, I spotted my mother; she was standing beside her friend. They greeted me and bombarded me with a barrage of questions as we boarded a vehicle.

October 2004
***

Now only a month after my mother informed me of her incarceration, I had to pack up all our clothes and remove them from our room in Tulse Hill because the landlord needed the room. I had no family in this country to rely on; so, I purchased two large blue plastic barrels with some of the one-pound coins that collected in the two-litre water bottle and filled them with my mother's clothes and shoes with the plan to ship them to Jamaica.

So, one Friday evening in October after school, I asked Joan's daughter, Swane, to help me pack up my mother's things. I had to empty the cupboard adjacent to our room to ensure that all our things were being collected. After rummaging through used bags and deciding what needed to be disposed of, one bag remained. Inquisitively, I picked it up. It was much heavier than its size. I pried the azure plastic bag open. I discovered a second black bag. I did the same. To my surprise, it was a gun! A revolver to be exact. It had a faint gold colour and looked quite tattered, as though it was passed through several hands.

Where did this come from? I eagerly took it to show Swane. Naively, I pointed it at her while I made shooting noises. I even pulled on the trigger twice! She shrieked in surprise. We both played around with it for approximately five minutes. I detached the barrel from the gun, and I discovered one bullet lodged inside of it. Then it hit home that I could have killed Swane when I fired the gun at her a couple minutes ago. In horror, I searched for something to remove my fingerprints from the weapon. I had only seen guns on TV shows—*Crime*

Scene Investigation, and all its franchises, were my favourite programs to binge.

Aware that it must have been illegally hidden in the flat, I decided to use disinfectant wipes to remove Swane and my fingerprints from it. Innocently, I found a pair of cleaning gloves, put them on, and washed my hands in them. Then I proceeded to wipe any prints off the gun and the bullet. After the removal of all fingerprints, I carefully placed the gun into several bin bags with the intention to dispose it. I was scared to hand it over to the police as I did not want to get anyone into trouble.

I had a feeling that it was the guy that resided in the single room beside my mother's and my room. He had left a couple of months earlier. I had no idea where he had moved to. I hid the bag in our room as I intended to return with help to transport the two barrels to Clapham South where I was temporarily residing. Early Saturday morning, before I started working with Jennifer in the salon, I contacted the man. I sent him a message to explain what had happened. He responded later that day. He said that he would come to the house to collect it.

However, around 10:30 p.m. that night, he decided not to meet me. Maybe he was afraid that I could set him up—I have no idea why he stood me up. I took it upon myself to dispose of the gun. That night, I pleaded with Swane to follow me back to the flat to dispose of the gun. She agreed to tag along with me for moral support.

As the house was located on an estate where plenty of children lived, I firstly wanted to protect these children from danger, so I placed my hands in gloves that I took from the hair salon. I placed my Jamaican flag (a miniature sized one that I used as a face cloth) and tied it around my nose and mouth to prevent any transference of DNA— even in the form of water droplets from perspiration that was being emitted from my face. Lastly, I put one of my mother's hats on to protect my identity.

I walked throughout the estate to determine where and how to dispose of the gun so that it would not be discovered by the children. I was unsuccessful; so, I kept walking. I came upon a bus stop that had a bin beside it. I used my initiative to dig to the bottom of the well filled bin and placed the bag there in the hope that the bin would be collected in the morning. I removed the gloves, but I carried them with me as I did not want them to be associated with an illegal weapon. That night, I prayed that the bin would be collected and that the gun would not be discovered, especially by any children.

CHAPTER 3

FAMINE

·····················•·•·····················

As I approached the decrepit, white ceramic shampoo bowl—discoloured and stained with black hair dye—balanced on top of an overused, repurposed, and worn-out black PVC leather reclining chair, I sneakily tiptoed past it to knock on the wonky black door that stood up to greet me. I heard no response.

"Chris, are you awake?!" I called.

No response. As this was a normal occurrence, I preceded to nervously push the door open.

I delicately and calmly walked past the man-made unstable glass wall that was filled with handmade jewellery; I noticed that the lights were switched on in the miniscule room behind this translucent wall. As I peeked around the wonky doorway, I was startled by Chris bent over a crooked blackened table, sniffing a line of white substance. He jumped up startled. Frightened, I jerked back. Chris quickly clutched his nose, brushed his trousers off to remove any leftover residue, and horridly ushered me out of the room.

In horror, and feeling dishevelled by what I just saw, I naively went and whispered to Yvonne about what I had just witnessed. Without any consideration for the repercussions that my confession would have on Chris, I confided in Yvonne. Yvonne then walked intentionally towards Junior's office—the salon owner—to tell him what I had told her just took place.

Seconds later, Junior stormed instinctively out of his office, with fury in his eyes. Junior—towering at six foot seven and an ex-amateur boxer—shoved the long-standing filthy and wonky black door causing it to fly in the opposite direction. Although Chris was over six foot, he was slim and bony, and half Junior's size in body mass; Chris looked as though he could benefit from a large plate of home cooking. Within a few seconds of Junior storming through the door, Chris' voice yelled out in terror. As the scream raced from the back, it startled the people at the front of the salon. Immediately, all three barbers ran frantically towards Chris' quarters to separate both men.

For the next thirty minutes, a commotion of argument exploded; this died abruptly when Junior marched out of the salon, frustrated with Chris' behaviour.

Business as Usual
***

"Nardia!" shouted Jennifer.

Jennifer reminded me of my mother. She was like my mother adjacent. She was my mother's best friend, or so I was made to believe. She was medium built with big breasts and lightly tanned skin like the paper bag in shading. She had a cute button nose with big bulbous eyes and a square face. She was unique looking in her own way. I thought she was exotic looking. We could not figure out what she was mixed with.

In contrast, Yvonne, Jennifer's half-sister, both sharing the same father, was her total opposite in every way. Yvonne was cool ebony and had small defined features: small eyes, a small and cute button nose, small lips, small in stature with humongous breasts. She had a kind heart that exuded like a halo hovering above her head. She walked with grace, elegance, and a sense of assurance.

"Yes, Jennifer!" I answered.

"Dean is here to get his hair washed and braided," she stated.

Dean was statuesque and towered over most men that entered the salon. Highly melanated, his skin was as deep as Wesley Snipes' and would glisten when met with water. He was a beautiful-looking man with a wonderful soul. I fancied him, a lot, but he was at least fifteen years too old—so I admired him from a distance, thorned between wanting him to be my father and my lover. I was yearning for acceptance and a sense of belonging.

As Dean was a client that I admired, I gave him the best treatment: wash service and braid. So, when I was informed that he was there for his biweekly salon visit, I was elated. Subsequently, I ushered him into a spare chair and delivered my best service. As I finished washing his hair, I handed him a clean towel and directed him to the empty chair. After the completion of an intricately well-thought-out braiding style, I preceded to trim the flyaways with smallish sharp scissors.

Consumed by the desire to provide my highest level of service, I continued to trim his hair intricately, but then out of nowhere, I felt hot air caress my ear lobe. I jolted in surprise as I flinched. In the midst of a second, I snipped a tiny piece of Dean's ear and blood started to stream down the side of his head. A terror-filled scream erupted from Dean's mouth and penetrated the stillness of the salon. Everyone grimaced in disbelief.

Jennifer rushed over in confusion. "What happened?" She scowled.

"KK surprised me! It was a knee-jerk reaction," I said as I frantically retrieved disinfected wipes to slow down the blood that was rushing from the top of Dean's right ear. "I'm so sorry, Dean!" I squealed.

He jumped out of the chair and pressed himself up to the mirror to inspect his ear. I reassured him that the cut was insignificant. After an in-depth inspection, he assured me not to worry about it—especially because he saw the event that led to his ear being cut. He paid Jennifer, thanked me, and exited the salon.

KK was equally as melanated as Dean; however, he was half his stature. KK was also half as attractive and half as articulate. In a nutshell, he was half the man that Dean was. Then again, I was being biased. Simply put, I was more attracted to Dean than I ever was towards KK. I simply was not attracted to him.

Jennifer kept persuading me to date KK. She claimed that he had money. She claimed that he would take care of me. I could not see it. I did not know how old he was; he looked around late twenties. Also, I believed that he had at least one baby mother, and I was determined not to be in anyone's collection. From where I was standing, he was a dope dealer; he spent nights on the street selling drugs. I had no intention of being caught up with that lifestyle, especially being sexually involved with someone that operated in that frame of mind. To be frank, I did not want to end up a statistic: a teen mother, baby mother, or a single mother.

I did not want to become my mother; this was my fuel and my motivation—becoming something better. It was my desire to break the generational curses that had wreaked havoc over the women in my family.

Jennifer tried to pimp me out on several occasions; she was the little devil over my shoulder trying to pimp me out. Jennifer was my mother's friend, or so I thought. When my mom was incarcerated, she promised her that she would look after me or at least advise me on walking the straight and narrow and being the best version of myself. What I saw was the moment that my mum turned her back, she switched up. She became conniving and evil—straight out evil.

I spent hours working for her in the salon. I would start work around 9:00 a.m., and most Saturdays, I would not leave the salon until 1:00 a.m. Sunday morning, and sometimes even later. During that time, I did approximately six braids and other ad hoc duties, such as washing and blow-drying hair. She never bought me lunch; she would buy one meal, eat some, and give me the leftovers. As I did not have any other form of income or individuals that I could rely on for food and other amenities, I would eat what she gave me. I had no other option; I was stuck.

"Talk to KK!" she whispered.

For about three months, she had kept trying to persuade me to date this man. I had to shut her down. I did not want to be prostituted or pimped by anybody; that was not my portion. I wanted to walk down Coldharbour Lane with my head held high, knowing that no one had any holds or secrets over me. Besides, I had generational curses that I wanted to break, and the first one that I was hoping to tackle on my list was not becoming a teen mother. I did not want to be my mother.

Remember, I was seventeen; how dare she tell me that I should get with someone in their late twenties with a rap sheet? What kind of person does that? After all, she was a mother of several children that were being educated in private school. Here I was being paid thirty pounds a day after slaving over several heads from around 9:00 a.m. Saturday to 1:00 a.m. Sunday mornings—thirty pounds! I never got a tip. She did not even buy me groceries, no clothing, and no food amenities. All I got was thirty pounds a day. I had to learn how to make that stretch for the month to buy lunch and go to school.

Over the course of about two years, she preceded to do the same thing—set me up with older, more mature men that she believed had money. She was relentless in trying to pimp me out, but I was determined not to become a statistic, and that kept me focussed and persistent. I had to be.

CHAPTER 4

HOSTILITY

C hristmas holiday was my refuge and my moment of hope. It was when I became engrossed in a reflective comatose state, and when I felt like I belonged to something greater than myself because it was my opportunity to be among friends - now consider to be my family. It was the chance to reset, unwind and reflect on how I, somehow, managed to survive the chaos of the year. This year was a particularly pivotal year as only four months ago my mother had been incarcerated, and even though this was a moment of gratitude and reflectiveness, I still felt submerged beneath water. I felt trapped in a transparent container at the bottom of an ocean, staring at the fish swimming outside of it, and looking up at the flickering sun rays hitting the surface of the sea water as I bounced around on the ocean floor. I was so close, yet so far, and I could almost touch it.

Noise escaped from the coach's speakers: "We are arriving at Bristol bus garage on the left!"

I spent Christmas holiday in Bristol with my aunt (my mum's friend)—I had done so since I was fifteen. This Christmas was particularly hard. I was in a room filled with happiness, but I was numb inside. I had my poker face on. I had to exaggerate emotions such as happiness because I was grateful to be experiencing the festive season, but a sadness lingered in my eyes. I was experiencing an out-of-body experience. I was watching myself; I felt fixated in time. I found myself drifting off continuously throughout the day. The effervescence of my baby god sister kept pulling me back into reality. She made it a bit more palatable. I rested in a cloud of gratitude to enjoy the festive season.

A week of reflection and gratitude was just what the doctor ordered. I left Bristol with a sense of hope; I was motivated and inspired that I could overcome any challenge that I may face during this uncertain season in my life. I had somewhat of a more positive outlook on my circumstance. After all, I still had my freedom.

Back in London, the air, despite being more polluted than in Bristol, felt lighter. I felt more inspired and that I could tackle any challenge that may arise. I was determined to do the best that I could with my A Levels. My intention now was to get the best grade that I could.

Readjustment
***

Walking towards Joan's house in Clapham South, everything looked the same. Opening the door and walking through the hallway, nothing had changed. I peeped into the living room where I was faced with furniture. I later learned that her eldest daughter, Cameel, had moved back into the house along with her three-year-old daughter. I was told that she was in between homes; she had to leave her previous house and was currently negotiating moving into her new home. I thought nothing of it. I shrugged my shoulders, made an indifferent expression on my face, and carried on.

So now I would be moved from the spare bedroom to sleeping on the sofa in the living room. I had to get in where I fit in. After all, I had no choice; it was either on the sofa or on the floor. So, I started sleeping on the sofa. I had just lost my constant: my mother, but nobody owed me anything, so I was grateful for having a roof over my head despite where I rested it. That was my truth.

One afternoon, after school, I walked into the house, and I was greeted by Cameel. She calmly and politely asked me to take a seat beside her on the sofa in the living room. Not thinking too deeply into her request, I followed her, and I sat beside her on the sofa. She stared me straight in the face, then calmly enquired whether I had ever been approached by her current boyfriend. I asked her for clarification because I was unsure what she was trying to say.

"Are you asking me whether Ricky has made sexual advances towards me?" I asked. I looked her square in the eyes and said, "No. We talk about school, hobbies such as sport, but never sex—in any form."

I was a bit confused because I did not know where that question was coming from. I asked her why she was asking me these questions, but she never gave me an answer. She simply repeated my answer to her, made a grunting noise and stepped away from the sofa.

I thought it was strange, but as I was going through my own issues, I had tunnel vision. My focus was to do whatever it took to stay afloat, and most days, I felt overwhelmed as though I was drowning. So, the last thing I wanted was to take up room in my brain with the relationship status of Cameel and Ricky. Months passed and I forgot about the conversation that had taken place between Cameel and I on the sofa that one evening after school.

Tension started to rise in the house. However, I was consumed by studying for my A Levels while dealing with being homeless, trying to sort my immigration status out, traveling to prison to visit my mother every two weeks with my Oyster travel card, and working on Saturdays at Jennifer's hair salon to finance my travel and food for the week. Simply put, I had a lot on my plate; I could not think of anything else or anyone else.

Late Nights
***

Tension built up like pellets on a scale, and gradually but without communication, my home environment became unbearable. It felt as though the world was resting on my shoulders. My collarbone became so much more pronounced over the months that running water would settle without human intervention. Many days, I felt drained and exhausted; the house was now a vacuum that sucked all the positive energy, shocking everyone that lived under the same roof. I felt trapped on the treadmill of life.

Saturdays were particularly difficult. I woke up at 7:00 a.m. and left out by 8:00 a.m. Arriving at the salon, I was elated with the expectation of uncertainty, knowing there was something positive to look forward to. It was the shimmer of light at the end of a pitch-dark tunnel. My return from the salon became later and later; I was avoiding the people in the house. I did not like the energy that greeted me there. And having undergone emotional and psychological trauma, I used avoidance as one of my coping tools. I stuck my head in the sand and pretended like all was well, even though in my heart and my spirit and my body, I felt the consequences and result of coexisting in a pressure-filled environment. I was losing sleep and I was losing weight—all I was eating was white hard dough bread soaked in milk every night. My inability to focus and sleep, negatively impacted by A levels.

This was my method for being independent because rumours were being made in the house that I had a boyfriend due to the late hours that I was returning from work. Every Saturday night, I dreaded returning to that house because I was unhappy there. I knew that I was not wanted, and so to avoid feeling rejected, I would avoid the place and the people altogether. Thus, my return from the salon was reaching as late as 2:45 a.m.

The Confrontation
***

One day after school, on a day like any other, I was simply going through the motions when I arrived at the house. As I entered the house and walked down the hallway, nothing had changed. The dining room was still filled with Cameel's furniture. I still slept on the sofa in the living room.

I dropped my book bag off by the sofa and proceeded to the kitchen where Joan, Cameel's mother, was preparing dinner. I greeted her and made minimal conversation. She was ok, I guessed.

After all, she was the reason why I was able to stay there while my mother was incarcerated. She was my grandmother's friend, and it was because of the kindness that she received from my nan when she moved into a new community—my nana's community—that she was now reciprocating it with me. With this considered, I was grateful for her.

As Joan had instructed me to do, I was in the middle of dicing some vegetables, when Cameel bolted through the kitchen door along with her daughter. She confronted me about sleeping with her ex-boyfriend, Ricky. She was close to my face and in a rage as she accused me of sleeping with him. I reiterated that he had not made any sexual advances to me. She did not believe me. I felt attacked.

Her mom braced her back away from me and exclaimed, "If Nardia said that she did not sleep with Ricky, she did not. Why would she lie?" While continuing to brace her away, Joan shouted, "Leave the kitchen, Nardia! Go upstairs!"

Horridly, I marched briskly out of the kitchen. I was overwhelmed and assaulted with Cameel's vulgarities. Confused and dismayed by her accusations, feared consumed me.

Cameel released daggers of hatred towards me. "You nah stay yah with me; you have to come out of Aunty Dawn's house. You have to come out tonight!" she belted through the kitchen door.

Blindsided, I had not realised that the house that I had been living in did not belong to Joan, but her eldest sister, Dawn. I was flabbergasted. I had no idea why she was accusing me of this. Venom escaped from her eyes like lava erupting from a volcano that was propelled towards me—I was guilty until proven innocent. Pacing back and forth in the hallway, I scanned my brain vigorously, and I could not identify what sexual advances or conversation she was referencing. My chest tightened with worry.

This is the last thing that I need! I thought. A sharp pain bolted from the back of my neck down the perimeter of my left shoulder. My legs buckled under the pressure. I immediately braced my back to the right side of the wall that the old-fashioned, rickety wooden staircase was affixed to.

Thoughts of *I have nowhere to go!* viciously swirled around my head like a category three whirlwind.

Nausea compounded the feeling, and the room swayed around me. Sluggishly, I crouched down to centre my equilibrium where I preceded to breathe short and shallow. *I have no family in this country. Why is this happening to me?*

The shouting that escaped from the kitchen sobered me up. Even though I was not 100%, I garnered as much energy as I could to move from my current position. I had to because the sounds were getting closer and more violent.

Cameel directed venomous statements. "You have to come of mi aunty house! You nah fucking stay here with mi! You nah tan yah with mi!"

I crawled up the rickety stairs to the bathroom hidden at the back of the house. I splashed some cold water on my face. A deep sigh sobered me up.

The commotion erupted downstairs. I grabbed my handbag, braced myself and headed towards the storm. Positioned at the bottom-half staircase, I saw that Joan was blocking Cameel from progressing towards me. As her arms were flailing, I saw protruding from Cameel's right hand, the largest bread knife that she obviously had snatched from the kitchen. Her mother body slammed her to the wall, so that I could pass them on the staircase without a physical altercation. As I squeezed past, my heart felt like it was pounding through my chest and my mouth felt dry. Sweat marks appeared along my armpits. Horridly, I marched to the front door and opened it, then made a sharp left turn towards the number 322 bus stop. As the bus stop appeared in my vision, a sense of relief embraced me.

As I placed each foot in front of the other, my thoughts trailed back to what just happened.

I cannot believe what just happened. I did not flirt with Cameel's boyfriend. He was a great conversationalist; we had great conversations about life, hopes, and dreams, but we never discussed inappropriate topics. He had always been motivational and encouraging, so I was flabbergasted as to where Cameel was coming from.

What am I going to do? I thought. *I have nowhere to go. I am stuck in a strange land with no family. My mom, due to her selfish decisions, is stuck in jail and left me to the dogs. Who can I trust? Where am I going to go?* I felt nauseous once more. A cloud of darkness hung over me. I was stuck in a season of darkness.

I felt as though someone opened Pandora's box and released it in my direction—blow after blow.

"I need a break!!!" I screamed as I thrust my head back.

With a deep inhalation, I breathed slowly as I stared at the sky. I closed my eyes as I attempted to evict the negative thoughts from my mind. This was cut short upon hearing profanities being shouted towards me. I flung my head to my right and was greeted by Cameel.

Cameel trailed behind me with her daughter, a broken broomstick in her left hand and one of my suitcases in the right. As she approached me, vengeance consumed her face; she wanted blood. She dropped my suitcase while spewing defamations from her mouth.

Suddenly, the bus rolled up to my feet. The passengers' eyes were glued on us like a scientist hooked on the workings of a chemical reaction. I felt as though a humongous spotlight was switched on us. Overwhelmed with embarrassment, I accepted defeat and with a huge sigh, I picked up my suitcase and boarded the transportation.

On route to Brixton, I was subdued by my emotions. *Here I am again, homeless, due to no fault of my own.* My heart ached.

CHAPTER 5

OBSESSION

W ith my face pressed up against the cool of the
bus window, my senses were excited as the
salt in my tears embraced the curvature of
my lips. Unconsciously, my tongue darted out to welcome
the emerging salt water cascading down my embarrassed
cheeks. Sharp pain darted across my enflamed forehead
causing my ever-persistent migraine to re-emerge, coupled
with bloodshot eyes; I was silently bawling at the back of
the bus. Too humiliated to make a peep, I simply sat in
silence as salty water poured from my filled eyelids.

I squeezed my eyes extremely tightly, praying that this was
a dream, and I would wake up in a new alternate universe
where I was much happier and had a family that cared for

me and loved me. Yes, I woke up. My mind took me back to relive what just transpired a couple of minutes before with Cameel. I was seated in Dawn's house, Joan's residence, back at number 32 Poynders Road. Thunderous noise exploded above me. Staring at the mahogany breakfront, the crockery and glasses were vibrating. The walls were shaking from the monstrous stomping that preceded above my head. In frustration, I stormed into the kitchen while hardly scanning my contacts for Ricky's number. I caught his name as the list rolled across my eye. Clicking on it, it rang immediately.

"Ricky, this is Nardia!" I spoke. "Cameel just tried to attack me!" I continued. "She has chastised me about us having a relationship. She claimed that we have been engaging in a secret affair. Where is this coming from?"

"Nardia, you don't even know what I've been going through since the last time I saw you," professed Ricky. "Cameel has been a thorn in my side. She has accused me of being out with you every time I came in late from work."

"Really!" I exclaimed in awe.

Where did this idea come from? When did it start? Why would she say that? All these thoughts were bouncing around my mind.

"Apparently, this was when you came to Crystal Palace to do my hair and babysat Venus, and they went out and I didn't go out with them," he went on.

"Where is this coming from?" I grimaced.

"She believed that because you were wide-awake when Kenisha touched you when she came into the room after returning from the party. From that day, she became more agitated and kept checking up on me by calling me when I was at work," he conveyed. "She even started to accuse me of meeting up with you on escapades whenever I worked late. I got tired of it and kept staying out even later which came to a head a week before she moved back in with you," he revealed.

I was flabbergasted. His revelation took me back to that day. It was unique and it was imprinted on my mind. I remembered that day as if it were yesterday.

A week before that day, I was pestered by Cameel to come to her house. She lived with her boyfriend, Ricky, and her three-year-old daughter, Venus, in a one room shared apartment in Crystal Palace. Upon requesting me to visit her house to babysit her daughter as well as braid Ricky's hair, a feeling of melancholy came over me. I did not want to visit. I had a sixth sense that was saying to not go. There were previous occasions where I had braided his hair and I had to literally beg for my ten pounds. I charged Ricky ten pounds to braid his hair because it was straight back, and he did not have much hair. What was most annoying was that his hair tortured my index fingers; it felt like wire being wrapped around my fingers whenever I braided it, and my fingers were always sore after. So no, I did not want to do his hair. Moreover, I did not want to babysit anybody's child.

Cameel nagged me for an entire week. She begged me to do Ricky's hair and babysit Venus because it was an important event. I believe a Jamaican artist was coming over and she had already purchased a ticket, got her hair and her nails done, and bought herself a new outfit. By the time that Friday arrived, I was worn down and succumbed to her pestering power. So, I finally gave in and confirmed that I would visit her home after school to do Ricky's hair and look after Venus while she and he went out. Also, I reiterated that I had work the next day, and so I would be leaving early Saturday morning to get to work at the hairdressing salon.

I arrived at the apartment around seven that Friday evening. Entering the room, to my left there was a single bed that Venus slept on and adjacent to that was Cameel and Ricky's double bed. Jam-packed in this double room was a dresser adjacent to the room's door, and a chest of drawers that had on its top a precariously positioned thirty-two-inch flat screen TV facing in the direction of the top of the bed that was placed along the overpowering lime green painted wall.

I felt confined and claustrophobic. I was restricted inside a room that was not built to house two beds and all the other furniture including a small fridge. The simple manoeuvre to get to Ricky was a struggle, dogging sharp edges of furniture and simply locating the limited ground space that was available to the visible eye. Braiding Ricky's hair felt like a gymnastic performance, half of me was positioned on the bed and the other half was hanging off the bed, held up by my big toe—it was a circus act. To make things worse, a pillar of smoke escaped from Ricky's brittle cracked darkened lips.

This is the foolishness that I can't deal with. I can't wait to not have to deal with this fuckery! I cursed in my mind. *How many times do I have to remind this man that I am asthmatic, and yet every time I do his hair, he smokes? Selfish! He obviously does not care because Venus is sitting right over there, and he is smoking in this one room with minimal ventilation.*

Rage rose from the pit of my stomach; I blurted out, "I need to go to the loo!"

I stomped off while asking Cameel for the directions to the toilet. Frustratingly, I threw myself onto the seat, while gasping for air.

"Arrgh," I groaned. "I hate my life," I smirked. *The bullshit that I must go through for ten pounds. It's not even worth it.* I collapsed tirelessly into my hands and screamed with heart wrenching frustration—for my life, circumstance and being forced to do something that I would not have normally done had I been given a choice. *Why me, Lord?* I thought while simultaneously taking a deep sigh.

"Let's do this!" I said, trying to pump myself up.

As I was leaving the toilet, Cameel sauntered past me to the front door to let Kenisha, her best friend, in. Kenisha came into their room and sat on Venus' bed.

I braided his hair with total conviction which took twenty extra minutes. My fingers were pulsating due to the rapidity in which I grasped the volume of hair. My focus was on getting his hair done within the quickest time possible. With relief from completing Ricky's hair, I made a huge sigh.

Happily, I went to relax beside Venus on her bed. Instantaneously, chaos ensued around us because Ricky announced that he was not going to attend the party.

"What do you fucking mean that you are not coming?" screamed Cameel. "Why did you make me spend all my money to prepare for the dance if you knew that you were not going to attend? Why did you make me ask Nardia to come to do your hair if you were going to do this to me?" Cameel stormed out of the room. She was fuming.

Venus became scared; so, I focussed on reassuring her that everything was going to be alright.

Kenisha, Cameel's best friend, pleaded with Ricky and begged him to change his mind. "Come on, Ricky, Cameel has been looking forward to this all month. She spent all this money to look good for the dance. You can't do this to her."

Still puffing on his spliff, Ricky was adamant that he was not going anywhere.

I do not know what happened. When I arrived earlier in the evening, he was going to the dance. It is customary for partygoers to head out to a highly coveted party after 1:00 a.m. And now at 12:30 a.m. from nowhere, he had done a complete one-eighty, and decided that he was not going to attend the party. As an onlooker, my focus was to prevent Venus from crying. She did not understand what was going on and rightly so. And I was simply watching an argument go from bad to worse.

The door swung open, hitting the edge of the bed. Surprised, I held Venus firmly in my arms as steam escaped from Cameel, and she lashed out at Ricky with venom.

"You are a selfish son of a bitch! I am still going out. I don't care whether you are coming or not! I am going and I don't care. I spent my money. I look good and I am going out!" yelled Cameel. "Come, Kenisha!" Cameel said assertively while simultaneously grabbing her silver sequin purse and heading to the door. She pivoted on her right silver stiletto heel, walked back to hug Venus, then said, "See you later, Nardia." Then out the door she went.

I was shocked to silence. Taking a deep breath, I stared intently at Ricky, trying to discern any element of emotions. Nothing. He did not budge. Like a picture, he was precariously fixated in the same position. Sitting on the edge of the bed in the same place when I was braiding his hair, with his blunt—now half the size of its original length.

It was late; I was extremely tired, and I had work all day tomorrow, so I went to sleep.

"Nardia," whispered Kenisha.

Instantaneously, my eyes popped wide-open.

"You're back already. What time is it?" I said with bemusement.

"It's 6:35 a.m.," she said. "Why are you so wide-awake?"

"I am a light sleeper," I responded as a matter-of-fact.

I moved over so she could get to bed. I looked over and Ricky was still awake and still in a foul mood. Cameel went to bed. I was wide-awake now and returning to sleep would make me late for work. I waited around for another hour and a half. Nothing. Nobody even bothered to give me my ten pounds or even mention anything about paying me for looking after Venus.

Venus slept all night, so technically, I did not babysit her, I argued to myself. *I am annoyed for not getting paid to braid Ricky's coarse hair,* I fumed. *I am never going to do his hair again! Never,* I promised myself while massaging my throbbing index fingers. I was snagged back into reality by a tapping sensation on my shoulder. My eyes bulged open. Sharp pain shot across my forehead. It felt like daggers being exerted towards my head. It must have been stress or dehydration, or maybe a combination of both.

"Where am I? Who are you?" I said to the man that shook me awake.

"You're at the final stop, Brixton. I am the bus driver."

I rose with conviction in my eyes like a demented puppet, grabbed my suitcase and marched to the salon. I did not know where I was going to rest my head tonight or any other nights, but what I knew for certain was that

Poynders Rd would never be an option. On my way to the salon, confusion clouded my thoughts; I did not know what to do, so I rang my aunty in Jamaica.

Tears streaming down my eyes, my migraine was still kicking my butt. I could not let this migraine overpower me; I was determined to stay focussed. I had to find somewhere to rest my head tonight and hopefully for the future. This and only this was my focus. I rang my Aunt Charmaine, my mother's older sister. She had a friend, Cecille, that had a house in Myatt's Field, up Brixton Road. She attempted to ring her and explain my circumstance to her, but she was unavailable. Still having no clear idea of where I would be resting my head tonight nor in the future, I asked Joan's second daughter, Swane, whether I could stay with her until my aunt spoke to her friend. She agreed and I stayed with her that night.

CHAPTER 6

HATRED

· · · · · · · · · · · · · · · · · ◆ · ◆ · · · · · · · · · · · · · · · ·

"Nardia!" yelled Jennifer.

"Yes!" I answered reluctantly.

"Come fi di food, mi finish with it," she conceded.

With a shrug, followed by the rolling of my eyes, I bitterly dragged my legs, putting one leg in front of the other while I walked towards her sitting in the salon chair that she rented from Junior.

After washing what felt like thousands of heads, more men's than women's heads, today was one of those days where I felt like I had been working nonstop since 9:00 a.m. After hours of working, the male head seemed to house more hair and not only more hair, but their hair was much coarser than the female head. *It could be because women tend to do much more with their hair than men,* I deliberated to myself.

Today was also one of those days where all my fingers, especially along the external curvature of my tortured index fingers, were throbbing. The invention of intricate designs necessitated the continual weaving of my fingers through acres of abrasive hair real estate, which resulted in swollen purple-pink fingers. Cartoon-like, they were closely mirroring Tom's fingers when Jerry would deliberately slam them in doors. I needed ice to relieve the pain coasting along my fingers.

As I slowly wandered in the direction where Jennifer was seated, a sharp pain shot up across my left groin. I buckled under the pain while grabbing my stomach. I immediately glanced up at the basic white clock, precariously positioned smack bang in the middle of the shop floor—far out of reach for everyone below six foot five—Junior's height.

Yep, I'm hungry, I thought. All parts of my body knew it. The sharp pains darting across my stomach were sure signs that my head would soon be the playground for hunger-induced headaches. It was a pain that would not retreat for at least four hours. Nothing worked: Paracetamols, Nurofen, or anything stronger could not cause it to cease. I would simply need to ride this wave until the pain subsided.

Inspecting the dishevelled, yellow polystyrene box, resentment consumed me. Jennifer promised my mother that she would take care of me, and here I was being gifted her leftovers. *I have never had leftovers,* I grimaced. Not even when I lived with my grandmother and we were dirt poor, I was still never bestowed another person's leftovers. *How could she?* I thought. *She does not even have the mere decency to buy an extra lunch for me. An extra five pounds was not going to break her bank. What kind of person does this?* I contemplated.

On average, I completed—from start to finish—five heads of braids. Intricately completed. With each customer paying an average of thirty-five pounds, I was bringing in £175 every Saturday. Yet every Saturday evening, she would roll up thirty pounds and disgruntledly hand it to me, way into the night—around 10:00 p.m.

Months after burning the prints off my fingers from them being bruised and overexposed to chemicals while working for her, I learned that Jennifer was sending her three children to private school in Jamaica. I was dumbfounded. Here I was struggling, trying to survive off thirty pounds a week from a woman that claimed she cared about my plight and well-being.

Unfortunately, at every opportunity, she was trying to pimp me out to any man that she felt had money: KK, the drug dealer; Dean, the chef / restaurant cook; and John, the seasoned pimp who was older than my mother. I was a seventeen-year-old left out to fend for myself due to the selfish acts and decisions of my mother. With no advice, inspiration, or motivation from the adults, I was continually being pressured by this woman to date older men. From age seventeen going on to eighteen years old, my focus was not to end up a single teenage mother like my mother and her sisters before me. I braced myself; I was determined to break this generational curse in my family.

I did not trust Jennifer anymore. All respect for her went down the drain when she tried to persuade me to let John drop me home one Saturday night. She was determined to pimp me out. As long as I had breath flowing through my body, I was determined to have full stewardship over my body and my decisions. The determination to walk down Coldharbour Lane with my head held high knowing that my body was not sacrificed for the pleasure of others, was a goal that plastered across my vision. How dare she give her children the best experiences on the gruelling labour of my harvest while exhibiting me for the highest bidder? How dare she? I hated her for that. All trust was lost, all respect. I despised her.

Now with each portion of food shovelled into my mouth, my brain started to work overtime to devise a plan to find a flicker of hope.

"There must be a better way. There must be!" I murmured.

I was determined to prove everybody wrong. I was determined to overcome old stereotypes. *I will overcome,*

I thought as the rice was squashed under the force of my teeth. I was determined not to consume Jennifer's leftovers anymore. As long as God blew breath into my body, I would be an overcomer. *Who is going to rescue me?* I contemplated.

My eighteenth birthday was swiftly approaching. I later learned that I had an aunt that resided in Maryland, USA—my father's half-sister. The only time I saw her was when she came to Jamaica to bury her father— my grandfather. I was seven years old at the time. I remembered that she had extremely long jet-black fluffy curly hair twisted down her back. She was ebony in colour. She was a mysterious beauty with dark brown mesmerising and kind eyes. I saw myself in her. I was hypnotised by her exotic beauty.

Through weeks of research, I learned that she was married with one child, a son. I wanted her to file for me. I explained my situation to her and begged her to help me. She agreed. My birthday came and passed. I made several attempts to speak to her and three weeks after my eighteenth birthday, she confirmed that she could not save me from my woes. I was devastated.

What transpired between her agreeing to help me and now? I contemplated. I concluded that someone deterred her away from her initial decision. The flicker of hope that I was clinging on to died. The opportunity for a better life slipped through my fingers once more. Extremely disappointed in her, I deleted her number from my phone.

"I am going to have to save me," I proclaimed.

Fired up with determination, I had a plan. I would ring social services and explain that I was homeless. They would have to provide somewhere for me to stay, even if it were a hostel or a group home. I located their number online and through sheer determination, I outsmarted the deviations of the social services' deterrence mechanisms, and I finally was able to speak to someone. I discovered that due to now being eighteen, I was considered an adult, and coupled with the fact that I had no documents— which were being held up at the Home Office for almost 3 years now. I had no rights to obtain any support from UK support services. Another blow!

"I don't know if I can afford to take another right hook," I professed.

The punch of bad news kept coming from all angles, and the blow from the social services was the punch that almost took me out. This injury built on the layers of resentment that I had towards the adults who were a part of my life to support me. *Why did no one inform me of the opportunities that I could have obtained when I was under eighteen? Did they want me to fail and end up a teen mother like them?* I spiralled deeper into a tunnel of depression.

HATRED

Despair Dawned
***

"Who do you think you are? Trying to be the boss of everyone. You are not the boss of me! You think that because you sent me an invitation letter, I must be indebted to you. I paid my dues, damn it!" quarrelled Yvonne. "You are self-centred and a narcissist. You think that you are better than everyone. You even decided that Nardia should only work for you when Nicey, (Nardia's mother's nickname), said that we should look after her. How disgusting are you? You could not allow her to work for all of us, so that she could earn more money. You know that she does not have any family in this country and still you selfishly want her to solely work for you."

With this revelation, all remaining hope, respect, and trust that I had for Jennifer went through the window. The last spark of hope dwindled and shrivelled in me. *Who can I trust?* I pondered. *She doesn't owe me anything. After all, my own mother disappointed me,* I despaired. Walls of protection sprouted.

Two years had passed, and my heart had hardened. I struggled in school. So many things happened. My resentment towards Jennifer grew. Rivers of water had settled under the bridge. I felt like an orphan . . . no one cared for me, so I had decided not to care about anyone. I owed no loyalty to anyone but me.

I started to work for Yvonne, and Annie, who was another hairdresser. Annie was the first one of my mother's friends I was introduced to when I arrived in the UK. She was the only hair stylist at that salon who was professionally trained and would regularly care for my hair. Unfortunately, the tension within the salon was unbearable and the silence was stifling. Peacefully working within that salon was no longer an option. An argument erupted every Saturday that I was there. Some customers stopped returning. I made an executive decision to quit; I needed greener pastures and bluer oceans for the semblance of sanity that still resounded in me. Working within this salon was no longer conducive for my spirit.

It was midsummer of 2006; I was at a crossroads. My desire was to survive, so I jumped ship without a strategy. I was sinking and I needed to live! But, before I left, there was one person's number that I wanted—Christopher, a beautiful Caribbean Indian, mother born in Trinidad and father born in Guyana. Five foot six in height, beautiful face and hair and a wonderful personality. We clicked.

I was attracted to him, but nothing would come of it. I did not feel worthy enough. Besides, I thought, who wanted to deal with my mess?

CHAPTER 7

STRIFE

L ife was a hamster wheel spinning through days of turmoil and the consistency of that prevailed. *Today's journey was particularly long,* I contemplated while exiting the 185 bus on Stanstead Road a few yards from the hair salon. *Saturdays come around too quickly,* I deliberated, sandwiched between yawns. *I hope Thelma pays me all my money today. I don't want to hear her excuses. Not today!* I thought. *What am I doing all the way in Forest Hill?* I asked myself. *It takes two buses and almost two hours to get here every morning. At least it's better than slaving for Jennifer,* I confirmed, reflecting on the harsh conditions under which I had to work.

"Good morning, Theresa!" I spoke.

"Morning, Nardia! You alright?" declared Theresa.

"Yes, I am good. It is Saturday—pay day!" I announced.

"She betta! I don't know what is wrong with Thelma! She stays watching her ex-husband. Can't she see that he doesn't want her? He travelled all the way from Fulham to get away from her and here she is pushing herself up into his space, trying to get him back. He does not want her," lamented Theresa.

I looked at her in agreeance.

"What does she know about the hairdressing business? She's not a hairdresser. She's not even a good businesswoman. Thank goodness I have a spare key, or we would be standing outside until she turns up, dragging her boys behind her," remarked Theresa.

"It must be hard though, travelling all the way from Fulham. I don't understand why she chose to open a hair salon on the other side of London. I'm not complaining. I need the job. I do appreciate that the shop is located on the high street, Stanstead Road, but it's extremely slow. Sitting around, twiddling our fingers, and staring at each other. It's such a waste of time, but that's not my concern. I turned up to work, but if nobody walks through the door, it's still not my concern," I concurred. I rolled my eyes and sighed as I rested my chin into the palm of my hand. "I have bills to pay, but I don't know how much longer I can stay here. I can't see this business lasting for another year. It's not fair on her or me. I need to be paid and she's not making any money to pay me," I professed.

"She is an idiot! Blinded by envy and jealously. She would follow her ex-husband to the end of the world if she could. Deliberately using her sons as pawns in the war of hearts. No matter what she does, he will not be taking her back!" Theresa declared. "He is too handsome for her and by the way, she is extremely insufferable—nagging and annoying. Any man in their right mind would run a mile. I bet once her sons get older, they too will be hiding at their friends' homes to get away from her. I promise that!"

"She can follow her ex to the edge of the world, I don't care. As long as I don't get caught up in the crossfire. It's the boys that I worry about," I affirmed.

"Good morning, ladies," proclaimed Thelma.

Theresa and I looked at each other knowingly with a half-cracked smile.

"Good morning, Thelma!" we responded in chorus.

"Did Rodrick pass by already?" Thelma asked.

Theresa and I looked at each other knowingly.

"No, he has not been around here," I confirmed.

Around two minutes later, Rodrick Junior (RJ) and Christopher came bustling through the salon's front door, both hauling a bin bag in unison.

"Lift up the bag, you mad!?" hurled Thelma.

My eyes immediately darted around to Thelma after she spewed corrective daggers in the direction of her sons. *I don't know how I would be if she was my mother,* I reflected.

Conceited Coercion
***

The day seemed to drag on. We provided service for a few customers, but we spent most of the time glued to the chairs and staring at each other. RJ was focussing a little too intently on me.

"If that boy thinks that I am going to flirt with him, he is making a huge mistake," I chuckled to myself as I slid off the chair to break his gaze. I rolled my eyes and smirked as I walked in the direction of the toilet.

Returning from the toilet, my focus was to avoid eye contact with RJ, and as I brushed passed Thelma, she declared, "You realise that my son has a massive crush on you, Nardia!"

I stopped in my tracks—"What? You are joking. I am older than him," I protested.

"Only by one year," endorsed RJ.

"Yes, one year too much!" I denounced.

What can this little boy do for me? My mother is in prison; I practically have no family in this country; the last thing I need is puppy love.

Weeks passed and Thelma persistently gave excuses as to why she shortened my weekly wages. I turned up on time and I did my work; all I needed was the appropriate compensation for it.

Unsurprisingly, she was doggedly focussed on hooking me up with her son. Eventually, she wore me down and I succumbed to her perseverance. Also, I talked myself into needing a little distraction. I knew it was not a relationship and I was not interested in one. I simply considered it to be a situationship. It might be a nice distraction to help me take my mind off my dire circumstances.

Easter weekend came around, and the salon was much busier than usual. This was the weekend that I would be spending with Thelma and the boys. *This is the weekend that RJ and I planned to do the deed!* I thought. The day went by swiftly, and the night rolled around carrying with it a weight of regret. It was my responsibility to accept the present or reject it. Knots brewed in my stomach. The stench of regret was chasing me.

Do I want to lose my virginity? Why am I considering this? RJ cannot do anything for me. He is seventeen and I am eighteen, and neither of us are in any position to have sex moreover have a child. My mind went straight to my mother being a single teenage mom. This recurring thought had been the natural contraception that kept me obstinate.

"Are you guys ready?!" questioned Thelma.

Jolted into the present, I answered yes. We loaded into her car and on we went on the route to Fulham, suspended in a sheet of UK house music. What seemed like ages later, we arrived at the front of her house.

"Home sweet home!" proclaimed Thelma.

My heart was in my mouth. I did not know what to expect with Thelma's house, but I knew what could potentially transpire a little later that night. Pouring out of Thelma's vehicle, I was instantly weighed down by a bag of towels tossed in my direction. Slowly walking behind, a waft of anxiety consumed me. Droplets of perspiration started to develop across my forehead. I felt nauseous. *Do I really want to be here?* Worry was pouring out of my pores. I remained humble and reassured myself of who I was.

"Welcome to my humble abode!" said Thelma with a mesmerizing, blinding smile and infectious charm.

Standing in the middle of the living room, colours and textures bombarded me, and for a moment, I felt claustrophobic. I was swamped by a hoard of stuff; ornaments and figurines were stacked up to the heavens.

"What do you think?!" Thelma enquired.

I gave the room a once over and was surprised by the precariously hung chandelier above me. It looked out of place within the dingy, overcrowded, and small room.

"It looks amazing!" I said while staring at Thelma.

She then went on to elaborate on how she came to have a chandelier in her living room. I did not hear much; I was overwhelmed by the vast number of things that she had forced into such a small space.

"Have a seat!" Thelma requested, while pointing in the direction of the one-seater white leather sofa.

She then handed me the remote and suggested that I browse the channels for something to watch. Then she went off into the kitchen to fix dinner. Forty-five minutes later, Thelma had rustled up some food in the kitchen and soon we were all gathered around the table, munching down the food.

What seemed like only thirty minutes later, Thelma went to her storage to retrieve her air-bed. It was single bed. She proceeded to fill the bed and her youngest son fell in line to help her as she went to obtain sheets and a pillow. She gave them to her younger son and ordered him to sleep on it in the living room. She then gently coerced us to relocate into the sons' bedroom—both boys shared the same bedroom.

RJ and I looked at each other knowingly. The palms of my hands heated up and became clammy. The boys' room was an extension of the living room and was overcrowded with stuff pouring out of all crevasses of the room. Their bed was a double bunk bed with RJ sleeping on the bottom. Feeling a little nauseous, I settled on the bottom bed.

Knots started to assemble in my stomach as I felt RJ's fingers climbing up my left thigh. He then turned my head with his right hand, and we commenced to kiss—disoriented, sloppy, and uncontrolled kisses. Inexperienced in our approach, we burst out laughing.

Instantaneously, we were surprised by Thelma's knocking at the door.

"Come in!" we commanded in chorus.

She sashayed in with chocolate pudding desserts for both of us and slipped her son something inconspicuous into his left hand. Then in the split of a few seconds, she disappeared out of the room. I enquired what it was. He confessed that it was two condom packets.

"What?" I echoed. "She is persistent with this."

"She simply wants us to be safe," he proclaimed.

I concurred in agreeance by simultaneously nodding my head and shrugging my shoulders.

We proceeded to kiss, and RJ started to caress me. Working his way up my trousers, my heart skipped a beat. Finding his way, his fingers gripped my buttons; a sharp erotic tingle rushed across the bottom of my stomach.

I jolted to my feet. I scampered out of the room into the living room. I rested precariously on the edge of the sofa. Uneasy and uncertain, I tried to stay awake if I could, but I could only manage having altogether a three-hour nap. I kept watching the clock in between every catnap. I desperately wanted to go home, but it was too dark to leave. *The moment it is bright enough outside, I will be out of here,* I said to myself. Around 5:45 a.m., I checked the timetable for the buses. I was determined to be on the first one travelling to Clapham Junction. The earliest bus was 6:15 a.m.

6:00 a.m. approached and I grabbed my belongings and disappeared through the door. I was out of there and no forces were going to tether me down. I did not want to be here. *The audacity of Thelma,* I reflected. *I bet if I were her daughter, she would not allow a boy to enter her house, wanting him to have sex with me. Life is so unfair,* I decided.

As I turned the corner towards the bus stop, I saw the bus approaching the stop. Adrenaline shot up into my heart, and I sprinted across the street, only just escaping oncoming traffic in both directions. I did not care, I simply wanted to get home to melt into my bed. I had only slept three hours in twenty-four hours: my bed was calling.

Monday Mourning
***

I arrived bright and early Monday morning for another day at work. *I don't know why Thelma does not let us work Tuesdays to Saturdays because we all know that salons are desert empty on Mondays,* I assessed. I approached the salon with a cloud of melancholy hovering above me. Through the salon window, I glanced at Theresa speaking to a gentleman who had his back towards me.

Stepping into the store, I saw that it was Roderick. He had come to the store to hand Theresa his copy of the store key as requested by Thelma because she had misplaced hers. Roderick was a handsome man; his face was a combination of Idris Elba and Shaggy, and he had the stature of Denzel Washington. I observed his face; it was distinguished and covered with a splattering of hair and a struggling beard. He had bright owl eyes that were mesmerising, coupled with a warm, hypnotising smile that exposed an uninterrupted set of teeth as white as piano keys.

I understood why Thelma was hooked. Roderick Senior was a seductive potion that forced you to pay attention, and then pulled you in; if you were not careful, there would be no escape. He was simply an exceptionally handsome man.

"Hi, I am Nardia, pleased to meet you. I am the new junior stylist here," I proclaimed.

"Nice to meet you too," concurred Roderick. "I just came by to drop off the spare salon key to Theresa as Thelma requested."

"I see."

"Will Thelma come to the salon today?" I enquired.

"No, she has an appointment, but she will be here tomorrow."

"Okay, ladies, I have to go; I have work. It was good to see you. Catch you both later."

"Bye bye!" Theresa and I said in chorus.

"Well, thank God, she is not in today!"

"Why are you saying that?" Theresa probed.

"I ran out of her house yesterday morning!" I revealed.

"Say what?"

"I was in RJ's room, and we were kissing, but it felt weird. My heart started to race, and I needed a way out. I felt trapped, about to do something that I would regret for the rest of my life. So, I grabbed my things and scurried out to the living room where I sat on one of her sofas all night into the early morning until 5:45 a.m. when the local buses started operation. I was scared to death of closing my eyes. To be frank, Thelma came into RJ's room and gave him condoms. The whole situation seemed manipulated and planned. It did not seem natural to me."

"What's wrong with providing her son with condoms? It is the right thing to do."

"Yes, I supposed. But it had me thinking, what if I were Thelma's daughter? Would she persuade a boy that I like to come home with me so that we could have sex? I doubt it. The point remains, I did not like her overall approach. It seemed biased and unscrupulous. It did not feel right within my soul, and I felt as though I would be unveiling something devious—uncovering one of Pandora's seven curses—STRIFE."

Surety in the Uncertainty
***

Weeks had passed and Thelma's dismissiveness grew. Resentment was displayed through vulgar and reckless comments and statements. Remarks on my immigration status were brought up in several inappropriate conversations, especially in conversations with customers. Every underhanded discussion was directed at me. On many occasions, I was forced to bite my tongue because even though the other parties in these conversations were unaware of who she was talking about, her sons, Theresa and I knew that she was throwing darts at me. As I needed the job, I just bite my tongue and dismissed her conniving behaviour.

One sunny Saturday in the summer, the sun stood proudly in the sky as time rolled by. This was quite unusual in the UK. We experienced, on average, three good weeks of sunshine in the summer. The presence of the sun made me tingle inside. Like a beautiful buoyant butterfly, I felt new birth. The mental and psychological experience of breaking my cocoon warmed my heart.

I will have a prosperous day today; I can feel it in my bones, I reaffirmed to myself. *I am a bold, bodacious, and buoyant butterfly embracing the kind embrace of the sun. I can do all things through Christ who strengthens me.* I affirmed myself the moment I exited the bus all the way the salon. *The crispy breeze of change beckons, and I am embracing it. No matter what transpires today, I will end the day on top. God let your will be done in Jesus' name. Amen.* A sense of peace cloaked me as I walked through the salon's door.

"Good morning, Theresa! It's a beautiful day, isn't it?"

"Morning, Nardia! How are you doing?"

"I am in good spirits today, Theresa. I feel a sense of calm and confidence about today. No matter what transpires today, it will be for my good. I am at peace."

"Well, that's good. Whatever side of the bed that you woke up on, you should try to stay on that for now."

I looked at Theresa and we both grinned gingerly as I skipped to my workstation. Customers started to pour in. Theresa and I operated like an efficient conveyor belt. I prepared the customers hair for styling and Theresa finished. We were more effective than a Chinese manufacturing plant as BBC Radio pumped current music in the background, maintaining an unspoken relaxed atmosphere.

Thelma strolled into the salon around 11:30 a.m., followed by her disgruntled boys hauling two bin bags of clean towels. I ran to help her youngest because he was obviously struggling with its weight.

"You didn't have to help him. He was just bringing it from the boot of the car around the corner."

I did not acknowledge her. It was crystal clear that the bag was too heavy for him. Also, I was in a great mood, and I wanted it to remain that way.

Her physical presence in the salon altered its mood. She brought with her a vacuum, diminishing pieces of the positive energy that pre-existed before her arrival. Gradually, the energy had completely depleted by around 6:00 p.m. in the afternoon. The flow of customers came to a standstill, and we ended up staring at each other in the salon.

I was ready to go home. The positive mental attitude I had at the start of the working day had now left me. My emotions were experiencing winter; at the start of the day, my emotions had been in the peak of summer. Aspiration, hope, and productivity were at their peak. I felt that I could bring to life all possibilities. Now, all those emotions slowing drained from me.

"What time are you closing the salon?" I asked.

"WE close at 9:00 p.m.," confirmed Thelma.

"Why wait until 9:00? It's approaching 6:30 p.m. and we have not had anyone enter the salon since 6:00. Why are we waiting so long?"

"We close at 9:00 p.m."

"That should be if we already had customers in the salon that we are servicing before 6:00 p.m."

"Do not question me; this is my business, and I will run it how I wish."

"Why should we work for twelve hours?"

"What is your problem with me? Don't tell me how to run my business!"

"I'm simply giving you logical advice. What is the likelihood that a customer will walk into a salon at 7:00 at night without an appointment?"

"I don't care about your opinion!" said Thelma dismissively. "I never asked for your opinion, so don't give it to me. Keep it to yourself."

"But, Thelma, Nardia's comments make sense. Why are we waiting in the salon for a random passerby to enter the salon and request service? It makes sense to shut up shop if by 6:00 p.m. we do not have any customers," lamented Theresa.

"I don't care what Nardia has to say. She wants to force herself into other people's spaces and dictate how they treat her. It's her way or the highway," Thelma protested.

"What is truly bothering you? It seems that something is bothering you," I asked Thelma. "Are you still mad that I popped out of your house before having sexual relations with your son?

You obviously had a sinister plan that you wanted to entrap me in. It is too obvious that you wanted me to date your son and use that against me for your advantage. You were trying to manipulate me when it was time to pay me at the end of the week. Legally, me getting with your son is illegal. Why would I want to get myself involved with this mess? Why would I want to be entangled with your family? So, you can wave it over me when it is time to pay me my full wages?"

I was fuming. I stormed off to the toilet. I was in a rage. I'd had enough—with her and this situation. I was sick and tired of being sick and tired. Theresa rushed in to console me.

"Diligently, I turn up to work on time. I work my ass off, and sometimes my fingers hurt for days after. All I ask for is my wages at the end of the week, without any excuses or a vendetta to manipulate me out of the full amount, which to be honest is not enough," I rambled off to Theresa.

"I know what you mean. It is extremely frustrating at times."

"Well, I have had enough. I am done."

I stormed out of the toilet and requested my full wages from Thelma. "Please can I have my wages for this week? I want it now, so that I can get home. I have had enough. I am done. Please give me what you owe me and find someone to replace me moving forward."

The entire event was a whirlwind. In the blink of an eye, the ordeal was over. I leaped out of the salon after receiving my wages; I gripped it tightly, took a one-eighty degree turn and went out the door. I stopped for a few minutes to catch my breath. Hope was slowly awakening in my heart like a flower blossoming on a bright crispy spring morning. *I don't know what the future holds, but I know that anything is better than this,* I reassured myself as I strolled quietly to the bus stop while nursing my anxiety.

CHAPTER 8

FAITH

I t was another weekend spent in Bromley. 23 Belvedere Road. Another weekend.

I arrived Friday evening, just in time to meet the lady of the household as she arrived home from work. I would weave her hair first. Whatever hairstyle she desired, I would have to make it work: a wig or weave. Thereafter, I would work my way through the other three girls in the house, doing whatever hairstyle they wished. I would not finish until Saturday afternoon, sandwiched between four or five hours of sleep on a sofa, usually in the living room. I had no option, I needed money to pay for my travel to college, and to buy lunch to eat while there. This had been my norm for the past two and a half years.

I hope my immigration status gets sorted out soon because I don't know how much more of this I can take, I reflected and rested on this notion. This idea embraced me at night and gave me the fuel that I needed to push through the present pain that bubbled up as my chest tightened. My legs and my waistline ached from being upstanding for over seven hours. A thin film of haze engulfed my eyes, and still mourning the dreams of attending medical school, a warm trickle of tears rolled down my cold cheeks.

7:00 a.m. Saturday morning, I rose and headed to the bathroom where I brushed my teeth and washed my face. I made myself a strong cup of coffee and released five Jamaican crackers into the mug—nasty, I know, but my belief is: don't dismiss it until you try it. After several gulps of the bitter coffee, it shocked me into focus.

I sat down in front of the dining table and rummaged through a blue plastic bag of two packs of 1B Xpression's synthetic extensions. I snipped, feathered, oiled, and brushed through layers of plastic to make it have the appearance of permed black hair.

Rianna finally woke up at 8:00 a.m., had her breakfast and positioned herself on one of the wooden dining chairs which was parallel to the forty-five-inch TV affixed on the wall. I concisely manoeuvred my way through acres of thick, bountiful cotton-soft 4C hair.

Hours later, my fingertips were red and pulsating. Most parts of my body ached, and I felt like my body had been put through the ringer. I was exhausted too as I was only functioning on five hours sleep within the last twelve hours.

At 5:00 p.m., I was ready to leave Bromley. I had completed my stint here. All the females in this household hairs had been completed—for at least the last six weeks. Resting my butt on the 136 bus, I made a huge sigh of relief. *At the start of this journey, the end always seems so far away,* I reflected on how I never knew how I had arrived at the end.

I need this money though, especially now that I am not working at Thelma's salon, I agreed.

Lord, I need a job. I just want to do braids, so that I can resit my A Levels if I need to. I prayed silently while sitting on the 345 bus heading to South Kensington. *Lord knows that I have been struggling with this whole ordeal of my mom being incarcerated and sleeping on family friends' sofas. The last two and a half years have required strong emotional conviction and your grace, Lord, please help me,* I pleaded internally.

As the bus approached Camberwell Church, a quiet noise instructed me to move from the right side of the bus to the left side. Without question, I moved. I sat at the front of the bus, and bright as day, there was positioned a sign saying, **"*Braidist Wanted!*"** Immediately, I pressed the stop button and exited the bus at the next stop: Camberwell Green. Fixated on the location of where the sign was posted, I was standing adjacent the shop—a chicken and chips shop.

"There it is!" For a few seconds, I asked God for confirmation. "God, is it you?"

Without waiting for an answer, I followed the stairs down to the basement. To my surprise, there was a small, snugged, perfectly imperfect functioning salon. As I approached the final stair, I took a ninety degree turn and I was pleasantly surprised when I was face-to-face with Cheque. She was a friend and a customer whose hair I had been braiding for the last eight months of her pregnancy.

My face instantaneously exploded with a flow of joy. Excitement erupted from my stomach that had been tightly wound a moment ago while entering the salon. Aghast, I made a beeline to Cheque.

"How are you?" she said, and then immediately started to promote my capabilities to Sandra.

"She is the girl that I was telling you about!" declared Cheque. "She is extremely talented and gifted. When she braids my hair, it lasts for weeks until I manually removed them from my hair—they do not fall out. You know how small I like my braids; she ensures that all the braids' sizes are the same throughout my head."

"Thanks, Cheque, for declaring my praises," I coyly said.

"When are you free to start?" Sandra directed towards me.

Sandra had an American accent combined with layers of a Jamaican accent thrown into her sentences. She was cool ebony in shade with a curly boy-cut hairstyle. Her skin was flawless—she was a natural beauty. She stood at five foot seven in height and required no adage to elevate her beauty.

"Now! If you would have me."

"So, what can you do?"

"Well, I have been braiding hair, in various styles and patterns, for the past three years. Also, I can braid in all sizes—specially with pick-n-drop. At the salon that I started working in, I would prepare the hair for weave by completing the foundation. In addition, I can perm hair too."

"Okay. Can you weave or complete a wig?"

"No, I don't how to do those, but I am open and willing to learn how to do both techniques."

Sandra slowly shook her head vertically and her eyes seemed to sway from left to right as she appeared to be processing the information that I just relayed to her.

"Take the last chair over there!" Sandra instructed as she pointed towards the other half of the salon.

It was separated by a wall that had a large section cut out of it, so that customers and employees could see both sides of the salon with the least hinderance. The salon was obviously makeshift. There was a great deal of equipment and materials stuffed into its miniscule size. I manoeuvred my way to the back of the salon where the chair that I was allocated was stationed.

The chair was tattered and aged, and its leather was peeling away from the upholster. Upon inspection, I noticed that the chair was unstable and rested on some stacks of old magazines. I ran my eyes around the perimeter of the space. It felt like a basement. The room contained five chairs tightly positioned within the space. There was three on the side where I was positioned, and two on the other side, tightly squashed in with a washing basin. The salon was compromised of two senior stylists, two junior stylists and one new junior stylist—me.

"Well, this is my new home now!" I acknowledged.

I stood in silence, thanking God, and accepting my new fate. I said a short prayer, knowing that he just showed up for me in my moment of need and not only did he provide the position for me, but he also provided an advocate for me. All I needed to do was show up. I exhaled a huge sigh of relief and a tiny spark of hope reignited in my stomach.

The salon was extremely busy. I did all the braiding for the foundations: weaves and wigs.

At the end of that day, I received fifty pounds. I had worked from 6:00–10:00 p.m. I cannot remember agreeing on payment terms. I was so overwhelmed by how quickly I received that role that I totally forgot to establish payment terms. *Look at God,* I thought. *I went from a salon a week ago where I was staring at Theresa's face, bored to death. Now, I barely get a moment to consume my lunch.*

Three months had passed, and I was overworked. The salon was full, and the crowd was overflowing out onto the steps; people were patiently sitting in order on each step leading out of the salon. Saturdays were the worst, especially when there was a dance or an important event or party. Sandra's salon was one of the hit salons in South London. It was the place to be. Sandra was in tune with the newest hairstyling techniques.

Working here was my first experience of navigating between different calibres of people: white-collar, educated women between 9:00 a.m. to 6:00 p.m., and ghetto-fabulous dancehall fanatics from 6:00 p.m. to midnight. When there was a huge dance on, we would be open until 1:00 a.m. on Saturdays.

Established Envy
***

Arriving at work one Wednesday morning in August, I came across a small crowd congregating outside the chicken shop. It was not strange to see a crowd, but the timing, however, was somewhat atypical. A crowd tended to exist after school hours for the secondary school children and on Fridays and Saturdays for the hair salon.

Today is Wednesday? I considered. Rummaging around my bag, I felt my phone and pulled it out to satisfy my concerns. *It is Wednesday; so, why are there people gathering?*

Upon approaching the shop, my eyes darted around where I saw Sarah and Rashida, the two hair stylists from Sandra's salon. *Where are they going?*

I glanced around a second time, and I spotted Sandra leaning agitatedly on the chicken shop's door that served as an entrance to both the chicken shop and the hair salon.

"What's going on, Sandra?" I enquired.

"They have quit their jobs!"

"What! Why!?" I grimaced.

"Envy, I guess. They didn't bother to consider how it would affect my business. They just packed up their stuff and decided that they wanted to leave. On top of that, they took some of my customers. Who, God bless, no man curse!"

"You guys can't walk in my shoes. I have more talent in my pinkie than both of you combined!" Sandra yelled at them.

The white of their knuckles was prominent while gripping their boxes of hair products. Sarah and Rashida continuously marched in unison into a salon two doors from Sandra's location. She avoided all eye contact and showed no emotion.

"Did they raise any concerns with you? Did they speak to you or give you any indication that they were unhappy? Was it the money—did they want a pay raise?" I probed.

"No, they said nothing to me," confessed Sandra.

Is she telling me the truth? Would she tell me the truth? I had been there an extremely short period of time and the only thing that stood out to me was that Sandra was bossy—it was her way or the highway. *Can I live with her dictatorship and micromanagement? It doesn't bother me; after all, people travel from all over the UK to come here for her. She is intolerable at times, but I would relegate that to her inability to stray from perfection. Yes, this is a highly stressful environment, but everything that is of great value is all built under great pressure. I am but a mere vessel and for me to leave this experience, when it is time to do so, I want to have acquired as much knowledge and skills as possible,* I contemplated.

I did not see this coming. Obviously, they were unhappy, but the sheer audacity to walk out of your job to then go shack up at your jobs' competition is extremely vindictive, I thought. Well, I knew that there were always three sides to every story. In this case: Sarah and Rashida's, Sandra's, and the truth. I was still unaware why they left, but they had worked for Sandra for over four years. It could have been their salary, or their inability to progress any further; it could have been anything. There was no point guessing; they were gone now. A reconciliation would never be possible. Whatever the reason that compelled them to walk out would reveal its roaring head eventually. So, for now, I would continue to turn up to work and give my utmost. This was a unique opportunity to acquire lifelong skills. I sighed and shrugged my shoulders simultaneously, then I proceeded to walk into the salon.

Two days later, two new stylists started working at Sarah's and Rashida's stations. Both stylists were Jamaican.

One held a senior position—Tamika. She was the same hue as Sandra. A larger-than-life personality, her animated face metamorphosed with her emotions and expressions. She had big, bright cartoon-like eyes that were in perfect balance with her nose and lips. The other was a junior stylist like me—Punkie. We were two years apart in age. She was petite with similar shade to Halle Berry. Her eyes revealed her Chinese heritage, and she had a similar nose and eyes to suit.

Punkie and I soon became close friends as we had many similarities: we were both the only child to our mothers; we were both Jamaican born, and both our mothers had us when they were teenagers. And as such, we both experienced quite tumultuous upbringings— being placed third in importance to our mothers' priorities (money, partner, us). We bonded on a spiritual level. Even though our explicit paths varied in detail, they were both extremely tasking on how we showed up in our lives. Her dad died when she was a child, and mine was merely a sperm donor—might as well be dead, I settled.

Sickness Reared Its Ugly Head
***

There was a misunderstanding between Tamika and Sandra, and it finally came to a head weeks later. It was a busy Saturday like no other. A big dancehall event was scheduled to occur later that night, so Sandra's salon was spilling over with customers aspiring to attend.

Tamika was slower than all the other hair stylists in the salon. Her excuse was that she suffered from heartburns, and as such, she needed to have a break every three hours to eat to manage the side effects. It was revealed during this explosion that Tamika was in fact six months pregnant. The entire salon gasped in surprise. Yes, Tamika was physically overweight, but I thought that was a part of her charm, and we accepted her as such. Her weight was never an issue; we accepted her the way she was, but when her health started to impact Sandra's pockets, it became an issue.

Sandra morphed into the condescending, over critiquing, straightener-clapping owner/manager who made you aware of every bathroom break that you took. She became the overbearing, micromanaging boss that was suffocating us employees. Taking time out to have lunch was a problem to her; she barely wanted us to take fifteen minutes break. Yes, she was a hard worker, but she spent a lot of her time gossiping with customers, and at times, I felt as though I was in a sweatshop. *Now it is becoming crystal clear why Sasha and Rashida walked out,* I pondered.

Two months later, Tamika was fired. The speed at which she could complete her work had gradually depleted. Over this period, she started to sit on chairs while providing a service because she could not stand on her legs. Her breathing became concerning, and customers started to raise their worries with Sandra. It was simply not a good environment for her to work in when taking into consideration that she was pregnant—almost eight months pregnant—coupled with the hair paraphernalia and flammable products and being cooped up in a basement that lacked air extraction. She was being exposed to an unhealthy environment for a pregnant woman.

I agreed with Sandra; the working space was not a healthy one for a mother-to-be, especially one who was on the obese spectrum and struggled with breathing problems. So, Tamika bid herself goodbye and we never saw her again.

My relationship with Punkie grew rapidly. With so many similarities, we felt like sisters. However, as time progressed, she would show up to work nursing a hangover or smelling of marijuana. It was evident that she struggled with substance abuse issues. It was not discussed; it was simply brushed under the carpet. Unfortunately, over time, customers started to complain, and if history had revealed anything, it was that Sandra would remove anything or anyone that affected her finances.

"I want to make you aware of what is being said by the customers. There have been complaints made to Sandra. I think you should take heed and fix up, because if you don't, you will be replaced."

Punkie acknowledged my concerns and made the appropriate adjustments.

Weeks had passed and Punkie and Sandra's relationship was blossoming to be more than an employee-manager dynamic. It was a bit secretive, but I figured if their relationship did not affect my role and position at work, then it was not my concern.

Last Chance
***

First day of enrolment was scheduled for the first Monday in September 2006. I somehow secured a place in Virgo Fidelis Senior Convent School, since I was eighteen years old—the upper age limit—although I would be turning nineteen the following month.

This is my last opportunity to obtain good enough A Levels so that I can secure a place in university. I can't mess this up! I reflected. For the last couple of months since July, I had been mourning in silence—crying in bed every night—to self-medicate the emptiness that lived in my heart and ate away at my soul.

In July 2006, when I was instructed to collect the results of my A Levels, a humongous cloud assembled above me and trailed me like a bad scent. Simply reminiscing now about walking to the office of my old school, Kingston College, to collect my results was nerve-racking. I had no one to lean on. No one knew that I was a ball of nerves held together with a thin cloak of a faith that said, "It will all turn out for my good." I rehearsed those words in my mind, but clutching to those words made me feel like an exhausted survivor who barely had enough energy to stay afloat on a raft that had been at sea for a month.

A nervous wreck, I could not be in the building with all those victorious students receiving the grades that they desired. Deep down, I knew that I did not perform well enough to garner the grades that I needed to get into university. And I simply could not pretend to anyone, including myself, that I had obtained the grades that I so desperately needed if I had not. The disappointment would be too great for me to fake. I would not be able to salvage the energy to fake it. So, I quickly accepted my envelope, hid it at the bottom on my bag and escaped away from the sounds of victorious cheer filling the perimeters of the building.

Too much of a coward; I needed some good news. The last two years had been nothing but emotional whipping. Bad news after bad news. The last thing that I wanted at this moment of heightened fragility was more bad news. I could not trust myself to be alone when I unveiled my results. I needed to be in a controlled environment. I was so far gone that I felt as though negative results on my A Levels would be the final straw that would initiate my mental breakdown. I was scared to death.

Walking back to the train station, I constructed a plan: the best place to discover my outcome would be while seated on the train. *It's the perfect environment,* I deliberated. It would be the best place to be because the sheer existence of people would prevent me from falling apart. *Yep, that's what I will do.* Standing on the platform of Kingston train station, my mind was on overload. All possible scenarios were dancing around my head: the best and worst outcomes.

As the train approached the platform, my heart was in my mouth, and it started to race. Sweat droplets perspired around the perimeter of my forehead. I glanced over my hands; they were red hot. At this point, I wished I had sweaty palms, but I did not; my hands would simply get hot and flustered. As the train doors came up, my legs buckled beneath me. I briskly scanned around for a place at the window with no one sitting opposite me.

Seated, I frantically gasped for air. I was dizzy. I simply needed to be centred, so I took some slow deep breaths through my nostrils and exhaled through my mouth. I went into a daze. I came to awareness three stops later. Opposite me was a white gentleman engrossed in some form of reading material.

It's now or never! What's the worst that can happen? I took the envelope out of my bag. I flipped it over once to assess it. White with a plastic covered peephole. Nervously, I opened the envelope. The results read the following:
Physics—D
Chemistry—D

Biology—D

Use of Mathematics—B

Information Communication & Technology (ICT)—Level 2

I was gutted! I thought that it was the end of the world. I knew the reason why my grades suffered, but people would not care, especially universities. I had been sleeping on people's sofas and experiencing emotional trauma from my mother being incarcerated for six years, coupled with the fact that I was here in a country where I had no family and no emotionally safe space. I had not been in an emotionally safe space to study. Functioning off white hard dough bread and warm milk, and tears every night, was not a conducive or nurturing environment to flourish and learn. *I have to say goodbye to my hopes of attending medical school!*

The one glimmer of hope was the B that I had obtained from Use of Mathematics. I smiled because I knew the majority of that was due to the pure maths modules—mechanics, algebra, and calculus. The same could be said for Physics—I obtained that D due to mechanics.

Ultimately, the circumstances under which I had to operate while trying to learn the subjects was not nurturing. Even though I was gutted that I failed, it would have been a miracle had I obtained a B in all the subjects that I studied. I genuinely wanted a miracle though, and a sharp pain rushed across my heart as it shattered into a million pieces. I was on a slippery slope of depression.

During the next three train stops to Clapham Junction, I underwent a spiritual battle for my mental sanity. I was on the verge of having a mental breakdown. Despite not crying and having a blank exterior, inside I was a train wreck. I fought with every fibre of my being for my sanity. This moment felt like that start of the end. I could have given up at the point of discovering my exam results and became another statistic. *What am I fighting for? Why am I struggling to walk a path not travelled by the people in my immediate family, locality, and community? I could simply surrender and become a baby mother from a Jamaican drug dealer. At least I would be taken care of to some extent,* I contemplated.

Exiting the train at Clapham Junction, I reasoned that no one in my family had walked in my steps before. But I was certain that if any of my cousins were in my place, they would fight for this opportunity. God did not bring me this far to leave me. Although, yes, I could not locate Him in my struggles, and at times, I resented Him. *Every night, I bawl my eyes out until I have a migraine, asking the same question: God, why am I going through this?* I would wait and nothing. No answer.

Every day since that fateful Sunday afternoon in 2004, I felt like I had been submerged under water—in a daze. I felt like I was inside a huge translucent globe that was holding me under water, and no matter how hard I tried, I could not get free.

As I strolled, I concluded that I did not want to be a statistic. My mother was a teenage mother, and her mother was a teenage mother; I would do everything in my power as long as I had breath in my body, to break this generational curse over my family. I would not become a statistic. I would be a graduate and I would, someday, marry and have my children within wedlock.

I wanted my children to have the life that I never had. That was my right. I was determined. Yes, I failed my A Levels, but I had a genuine reason why this happened. The circumstance was outside my control. Once there is life, there is hope. I would find a way to retake them.

Approaching the entrance, I stood for a millisecond and absorbed the sheer grandeur of the building: Virgo Fidelis. It was something out of a *Harry Potter* novel. Distinguished, historic, and stunning. An all-girls school that ironically was located across the road from my secondary school, Norwood School. This school started from preparatory (preschool) through to sixth form. I was here to attend the sixth form. The name of the sixth form was called Virgo Fidelis Senior Convent School. The oldest you could be to attend was eighteen years old.

With minimal documents, I would not be able to register into the educational system. While I was studying at Kingston College, I used my mother's travel documents because at that time I was still underage. Now that I was eighteen, and my mother was in prison, I was not able to use her details to register into a course. One of my Jamaican classmates' mother worked at the school as a cleaner. She had a good relationship with one of the long-standing teachers in the sixth form. She was able to put in a good word for me and persuaded her to sign me up in the school. Thank God for her. Lord knows I did not even know where my documents were, especially my passport, which I hadn't seen since the autumn of 2003.

The immigration system in this country was spiteful, especially biased against Jamaicans and some African countries. I believed that they deliberately dismissed our applications and let us wait the longest time frame possible before they considered our cases, and nothing would change that belief. I knew of people that had been living in the UK for over ten years, awaiting the results from the immigration system—they were waiting their lives away.

With a quiet confidence, I strolled into the registration office. It was dark and dingy and smelled ancient as it was comprised of mahogany wood. For me, educational institutions sprung hope and new possibilities. It reminded me of a flower spudding on a crispy, mildewed spring morning. After signing my name onto the required documents, hope cuddled me like a safe secure loved one who wanted the absolute best for me. I felt reborn; it was my second and final chance to smash my family's generational curses, one opportunity at a time.

Afterwards, I merged with a group of six formers as we were led around the school for an introduction. Quietly I followed, and for every room I came across, I repeated this question in my mind: *Is this where I will leave my mark?* The thought electrified me, and butterflies floated around my stomach. I was elated. I was experiencing the same feeling that I felt when I went to Kingston College to register before my mom went to prison. Even though the tunnel was still dark, I felt change coming. The glimmer of light was expanding, slowly, but gradually. I sensed the widening of the flood gates. Expectation danced in anticipation of the greatness of new beginnings. I was screaming with pleasure on the inside.

Virgo Fidelis turned out to be a mirror image of Sandra's salon. Here I was being encouraged to go out of my comfort zone through challenges. I joined the debating team through a sheer willingness to people please. My business teacher oversaw the extracurricular activity, and one day, she had to leave. She asked me to step in to help her momentarily until she resolved her urgent matter. She returned towards the end of the activity. It was scary, but I pushed through. I felt better for enduring the chaos. The following week, she requested me to join the debating team panel. It was challenging, but I embraced and trusted the process, and at the end of the activity, being a part of debating team did not appear to be as daunting as I initially believed. In the classes after that, I was actively involved in preparing the members in elements of debating, from researching through to constructing and the delivering an argument. I enjoyed that process.

I still had hopes of possibly attending medical school. High calibre institutions would require you to take A Levels in one sitting, but I considered the second-rate universities. With this belief, I applied for a two-week work experience at Lewisham University Hospital. I secured the position—another beacon of hope. God was speaking to me; he was making a way. I felt inspired. The experience was transformational. I witnessed surgeries both within the outpatient and inpatient areas of the hospital. I stood beside medical students in the operating room and observed them remove a patient's cancerous intestine. It was mesmerising and I enjoyed every moment of the experience.

At the end of the two weeks, I had a one-to-one reflection with the head surgeon whom I shadowed for much of the time. He asked me what my purpose was for wanting to become a doctor. Genuinely, I did not have a warranted answer. I knew I wanted the "Dr." in front of my name. I knew I wanted to make a difference with my life. However, having listened to the head surgeon, who I believe was in his early forties, saying that he only recently started dating someone approximately two years ago, turned me all the way off this career path. I made up in my mind that if I were to commit my life, my existence, to this vocation, I would spend my life single. That scared me. If I knew nothing else, I knew that I wanted to be a wife, and yes, I want to go down in history as making a difference, but for now that was not in medicine—it could not be.

As I walked out on my last day to the bus stop that stood in front of Lewisham Hospital, I clung to my certificate of completion and felt deflated. I was no closer to having clarity than when I had started this work experience. I felt as though I wasted the last two weeks. The only thing I was clearer and more certain about was that medicine was not the vocation for me. I was disappointed because I had been through so much to get to this point, only to realise that I could possibly be extremely unhappy following my dreams. Revelation stung like an unexpected slap across my face. I decided to take the weekend and reflect on my next steps. I would need to start thinking about which universities to apply to and what subject I wanted to major in.

Months passed, and managing school and work were becoming my new normal. If I were not at school, I would be at work; the only free day that I had was on Sundays and I did not have the luxury of sleeping in. This was because when you sleep on someone's sofa, you need to be up before they wake up. It had been years of operating on empty; I had been functioning on scarcity since 2004. I had been emotionally, mentally, and physically exhausted, but I did not have the time or the mental capacity to be frustrated and angry about it.

Every second Sunday, like clockwork, I would visit my mother at High Down HMP in Sutton. It never became any easier. I was on my own, venturing out to visit my mother—the woman who put me in this predicament through her own selfish actions—and now I was the one that must provide emotional support for her. This journey felt like emotional torture—an open wound that could not get the chance to heal. Walking solely past those humungous security guard dogs did not help either.

One of my rocks had been my half-brother, Fenton —my father's son. He had called me every week since my mother's sentencing. On many days, he had to pick me up off the metaphorical ground and speak life into me when I emotionally and mentally hit the wall. Another source of my strength came from my aunty—one of my mother's sisters—Charmaine. I thanked God for her. She had to scratch me off the ground and spiritually build me back up when all my faith seemed to dissipate under the pressure of my circumstance.

Time had elapsed, and I had invested hours of time researching to find my new career path. Seeing as I would be the first in my family to set foot in a place of higher education, I was venturing into new territories, and I did not have a frame of reference. One statement that stuck with me though was my biology teacher professing that we should always attend the best institution for the subject that we wanted to major in. That statement resonated with me, and I adhered to it. I applied to CASS Business School, in London; a business school in Birmingham; and two others.

Results day conjured up similar emotions like what had transpired in Kingston College. Now situated in a smaller institution, one could not hide. There was no place to hide from humiliation because most people knew each other. I was mortified and had extraordinarily little sleep the night before. Shattered, I simply wanted to grab my envelope and slip through one of the slits through the creaky floorboards that existed throughout Virgo. I stood in front of the registry office. We all had to wait patiently for every other sixth former's name to be called alphabetically until it got to yours. My heart was in my mouth as I waited. My lips were chapped as my throat thirsted for water. Fear paralysed me and I was glued to the ground, unable to pull my legs away from the crooked old-fashioned Perspex-glass window that separated us from the registry office.

My name was one of the names that always got called last. I was in emotional tatters by the time my name was bellowed through the window. At this point, most students were bouncing off the walls, elated that they had obtained the grades that they needed to get into university—whether that be their first choice or otherwise. I was confident that I had performed much better than the last time, but still had a flicker of doubt. I needed ABB to get a place in my first choice—CASS Business School on Old Street, London. I was not sure whether I had obtained it. Any other grade would mean that I would have to relocate to outside London.

"Samantha White," parroted a second teacher in the fourier where we stood awaiting our results.

I was jolted to reality with a pat on my shoulder. "Sam!? Your name is being called," stated Audrey.

Audrey was born to Ghanaian parents. She was five foot seven—modelesque with thick voluminous hair sprinkled with grey hair. She had explained that her hair had been turning grey since she was sixteen years old.

"Thanks, hun."

Nervously, I dragged my legs to the window to accept my envelope. I was too scared to open it there, so I quickly escaped to the bus stop. I was sheepishly looking around to ensure that I did not recognise anyone from my form. Too anxious, I jumped on the 417 heading to Crown Point to disappear from the overflow of students pouring out of the school. Once there, I switched on a 196 going towards West Norwood. Relieved that I was in the clear, I switched buses at the West Norwood bus garage by boarding bus 2. While relaxing on the bus, I felt the confidence to open the envelope. My results read:

A Levels: Mathematics—A

Biology—B

Chemistry—C

AS Levels: Business Studies—C

Much better than the prior round, but still a little disheartening because I knew that I could have achieved ABB. Disappointed, I was going to have to start preparing for my adventure outside London. *What does it matter anyway?* I deliberated. I was still awaiting my documents from the Home Office. At this moment, my life was held in limbo. I did not get my first choice—CASS Business School.

On Sunday, the same week, I was rummaging through my post where I discovered two letters. One that was received about five months ago and the other a month ago. Both letters were from two of the universities that I had applied for—my first and fourth choices. I frantically read my first choice and it stated that I had received an unconditional offer and a similar statement was made by my fourth choice. I was elated. I was experiencing emotional somersaults in my stomach. Finally, something that I truly desired deeply had come through. Tears welled up in my eyes.

CHAPTER 9

RENEWAL

Months of quiet hidden communication between Punkie and Sandra had now been revealed. Punkie was merely helping to design Sandra's new salon. She had secured the empty space opposite to the chicken shop. In comparison to the basement where we were initially located, the dimensions of this new premise were approximately four times the size. It was enormous, to say the least. The new salon was at the bus stop—Camberwell Church Street—perfect for indirect marketing as commuters' faces would be fixated in the direction of the salon whenever the bus stopped.

Upon entering the salon, the front mirrors were prominently and positioned at eye level to captivate passersby. Entering the salon, one would initially be greeted by a sleek black receptionist desk decorated with freshly cut, long-lasting, neutral-toned flowers. Adjacent from the desk were five grandiose approximately forty-eight-inch sized imported mirrors and three on the side of the desk. Two pristine imitated chandeliers were positioned centre stage on the ceiling. The décor was draped in black and complemented with black tiles. Following the salon through to the back were positioned seven blow-dryers and a minuscule glass coffee table filled with reading materials: novels, gossip magazines, and hair-related magazines. Moreover, a small dorm fridge was precariously positioned on the far end of the work surface, and opposite this was positioned two wash basins, exquisitely designed for a wonderfully relaxing washing experience, and impeccably rolled clean black towels.

Since receiving my A Levels and acceptance into university, I was mentally checked out of working in hair salons. I was approaching twenty, and I was eager to start my career path. I was frustrated and tired of existing around low gravitationally-thinking people. All they were concerned about were designer clothes, men, and money. I was simply going through the motions to pay my bills and immigration expenses. I utilised this space out of sheer necessity, and as such, I stuck out like a sore thumb.

Two years had passed, and I was playing the long game—the Home Office needed to hurry up. I was tired of operating in a role where I did not want to be. This morning, depression had come knocking, and before I could check the door, a small remnant was liberated, and now melancholy was accompanying me today without my welcome.

As I exited the 345 bus, I popped across to the barbershop, opposite to collect the spare key. I approached the salon door and saw a loyal customer—a law student who resided in Essex and commuted here every six weeks to get her hair done. I acknowledged her, unlocked the door, and welcomed her in to have a seat. Almost immediately, a distinguished lady entered the salon. She did not acknowledge me or introduce herself, so I proceeded with perming my customer's hair. Looking through the mirror, I saw that she sat a customer down and proceeded to perm her hair. She swiftly swooshed the perm through the customer's hair and five minutes later, she approached me and instructed me to wash the perm out of the customer's hair.

I said, "I beg your pardon?"

Bodaciously and unapologetically, she repeated her instructions.

My customer belted, "She is perming my hair!"

She recounted, "I will finish it."

Reluctantly while rolling my eyes, I directed the lady around to the wash basins. Visibly annoyed, but still trying to maintain professionalism, I dutifully neutralised the customer's hair, brought her back to the front of the salon, and sat her in the chair.

This woman, who I now presumed was perhaps the new hairstylist (with no manners or decorum) had probably started yesterday on my day off—Tuesday. Waiting on her to finish with my customer, she glanced at me in the mirror, and once more requested me to wrap the customer's hair. At this point, I was fuming. I wrapped the customer's hair, placed her under the hair dryer and recommend something for her to read.

Once more, I returned to the front of the salon to view my customer. She was my customer because she came all this way from Essex to get her hair permed and weaved by me, no one else. Once I arrived, this new hair stylist instructed me that it was ***her customer's*** hair. I did not acknowledge her. I simply took my customer around to the back to wash her hair. While I was around there, the customer was visibly annoyed. Then she came around to our location for no apparent reason. Not acknowledging her, I kept focussed on my customer.

Returning to the front of the salon, I blew her hair dry and advanced to prepare her hair to be braided for the installation of her extensions. This lady went, once more and permed someone else's hair while in the middle of styling her previous customer. When the third customer was ready for her hair to be washed, she instructed me to do it.

The customer that I was with blurted out, "She is doing my hair! I came all this way for Nardia to do my hair and I have exams to prepare for, so the faster I leave here the better it is for me!"

I smiled and proceeded to provide the customer with service. The customer was extremely agitated, and I tried my best to manage her frustration by starting conversations to get her mind off the blatant disrespect of the other stylist. I was still yet to be officially introduced to her, and as such, I did not know who she was. Within two hours, the customer's hair was completed, and she loved and appreciated my efforts. She paid and exited elated. I apologised, once more, for the disruption and gave her an open invitation to return at her next convenience.

As the day progressed, more employees arrived and other customers too. At the end of the day, tension started to expose its nasty head in the salon, and nothing of significance was discussed. I understood, through indirect communication, who she was and the role she played. Sandra, at this point, was five months pregnant, and she needed a senior hairstylist to rise to the occasion so that she could take a back seat. The salon was booming: seven hairdressers of varying capabilities; two nail technicians; and one beauty personnel who performed the eyelash extensions, eyebrow shaping, etcetera.

Stubborn Strife

***

A month later, the salon had separated into cliques. The employees were all operating in their own microsystems with their own distinguished sublanguage. Chronically the outsider, I tended to focus on the customers and delivering the best service that I could. My focus was solely on ensuring that every client got their monies worth.

As I had been a constant in this salon for over two years now, customers were aware of the quality of work that I provided. And due to this, most—if not all—customers would pass under my hands before they went to the senior stylist to be finished. As all the junior stylists were aware of this, they started to become slow, and the quality of their work dwindled. They lacked conviction and interest in my perspective, and they knew that no matter what, Sandra would instruct me to fix their shortcomings and low calibre work.

Even though I hated working there and I was disheartened with doing people's hair, it was instilled in me by my maternal grandmother that "Anything that is worth doing, should be done well the first time." Also, my aspiration of perfectionism, and respect for my customers' money, would not let me stray away from the level of quality that I had mastered for myself.

Months had passed, and I had felt overworked and undervalued. While everyone had the luxury of taking thirty minutes for their lunch break, I hardly received fifteen minutes to eat. Most days, I could only eat half of my lunch with no grace period to digest what I had consumed. I did everything, from braiding pick-n-drop, perming, weaving, wigs—all the techniques. Oftentimes, I was braiding the foundation for each customer, then transferring them to other junior hair stylists to weave. When most of the hair stylists had the opportunity to fashion long colourful nails, I was not allowed because I needed to be able to braid hair. The other hairstylists had the leeway to dress outside the salon's uniform requirements (black trousers and white professional tops), but I could not. I felt like Cinderella at times.

My overcommitment to satisfying everyone's needs except mine came to a staggering halt when I learnt that I was being paid the same daily rate as all the other junior stylists. This was even though they did not do significantly half the amount of work I did, not to mention the quality of work that I delivered. I expected not to obtain the same rate as the senior stylists, but surely not the same rate as the other junior stylists because I was involved in training them, and I picked up the pieces when they could not be bothered to improve the quality of their service. I emotionally checked out. I thought that if Sandra could not see it in herself to raise my salary to reflect the level of work that I was delivering, I would not make mention of it.

I simply started to put me first. I started to take my full thirty minutes to eat lunch and when she or any other stylists would rush me, I would answer with an assertive tone, "I am on my lunch break." I did not feel any way about it. Also, I decided to slow down on my turnover time. Before now, I was expected to complete a full head of weave (from start to end) within forty-five minutes and the same for a wig. If you ask anyone within this field, this is extremely difficult to accomplish as this procedure is a bespoke service. I was pushing myself to the extreme and I was not being compensated admirably. So, once I learnt that I was not being compensated fairly, I checked out.

Jealousy
***

A day after my birthday, I missed a phone call. It was from a landline; I did not think much of it. I acknowledged this missed call approximately 11:30 that night. As I unlocked my phone, a constant pressure pulsated across my forehead. The soles of my feet were sore and felt as though I had stood on coal for the last three hours. As my index finger scrolled over my voicemail, my waistline buckled under the pressure: a constant reminder of continuously standing on my feet for over twelve hours. It felt as if

I had pinched nerves close to my spine. The pain was excruciating and bulldozed its way down my legs. Waiting at the bus stop was an extremely painful task as tremors engulfed me like an individual trying to wean themselves from substance abuse. Pure exhaustion.

Today was a hectic day—a momentous dance. I was working like a dog. And now I was enduring the side effects coupled with being on the brink of starvation. Balancing my cold half-eaten lunch and my phone, I desperately needed a seat. I decided to not listen to the voicemail until I was sitting on the bus. I was a bag of nerves, and too concerned that this voicemail could be my solicitor. Moreover, I did not know whether I could handle the Home Office rejecting my application at this moment. Unfortunately, this had happened twice before. To be frank, I did not know if I had the resilience to push through a third rejection, especially knowing that my future awaited. University was to commence, I had a career and goals to aspire to, and most importantly, familial generational curses to break.

A 345 bus rolled up to my feet. Cautiously, I boarded and found the nearest empty seat visible. With a deep inhalation, I dialled the voicemail number. Waiting with abated breath, a colossal number of scenarios bounced around in my mind, from the worst to the best, and many varied combinations. Tightly squeezing my eyes, I wanted to minimise the doubts and fears that held my emotion at ransom. After a few minutes, they were quiet enough to be able to listen intently.

I was correct, it was my solicitor. My heart began to race. I tried to listen but worry fogged my focus and no matter how hard I tried to listen, I could not hear the words clearly. I felt submerged below water—the words that escaped from the phone sounded far way. I switched the phone off. *I'm too tired for this.* I sighed. *I'll listen first thing tomorrow,* I decided.

Sluggishly, and cautiously, I moved through Myatt's Field, a community that taxis drivers were reluctant to venture through. Gangs ran rampant throughout the estate, preying on young boys. At times like this, I thanked the universe that I was not of the masculine persuasion.

Finally making it in the house, I dragged my stuff to the living room, where I was temporarily sleeping as all the rooms had been claimed. Entering the room, I headed to the dining table where two folded sheets were left on one of the chairs—located the furthest from human usage. Grabbing both nonchalantly, I used the thinnest sheet to cover the leather of the black sofa, and the thicker sheet to cover myself from head to toe.

The next day, I rose like any other day—bright and early before anyone else in the household—to hide the sheets and tidy the living room. I did this like clockwork, no matter the season. While the house was quiet, I figured this was the best opportunity for me to listen to my voicemail. So, I rummaged through my handbag and anxiously listened.

"Good afternoon, Samantha. This is Mrs. Jeckodi, your solicitor. I wanted to speak to you directly, but this is the best I can do for now. It's GREAT NEWS! My darling, you GOT IT!!!"

I threw the phone out of my hand. Years of suppressed emotions erupted. I started to jump around the room. The great thing was the living room was located on the ground floor, so no one would hear me running around like a lottery winner. This transpired for a couple of minutes, until I was dizzy. I tried to console myself on the sofa, but I bawled my eyes out until I ended up with a long-lasting migraine. While lying flat out on the sofa trying to console myself, I replayed the voicemail.

Mrs. Jeckodi continued. "Pop by the office on Monday to collect your documents, and congratulations again!"

I was in a dizzy haze, and for most of the morning, I nursed my migraine. I did not care; I was clouds high, floating above the Earth's atmosphere. That was where I wanted to be for now.

Later that day, I told Sandra that I needed half day off to go my solicitor who was in East London. I was introduced to her because she was my mother's legal aid solicitor. While my mother was discussing her situation with Mrs. Jeckodi, she had brought my circumstance to the forefront. After reviewing my case, she agreed to take my case on under legal aid. By the time I was introduced to Mrs. Jeckodi, I had lost all hope in solicitors. On two occasions prior, I was robbed and misleaded by two unscrupulous solicitors. Even while discussing my circumstance with Mrs. Jeckodi, I had no faith in her. I prayed on it, and I made peace with the whole issue. Whatever the outcome, I knew that it would be done for my good.

Approaching Mrs. Jeckodi's office, a massive sense of calm consoled me. Directed by the receptionist, I sat patiently in the waiting area until my name was announced. Giving a quick glance around, there were quite a few melancholy people with ghost-like faces.

"Samantha White," echoed Mrs. Jeckodi's voice.

I leaped to my feet, butterflies dancing around my stomach. I sashayed to her office. I was floating on air, and I had a fixated smile plastered on my face.

"Good morning, Mrs. Jeckodi!" I proclaimed.

"Hi, Samantha! Congratulations, I am so happy for you. You look like a picture! Night and day to how you looked last year."

I agreed with her. "Mrs. Jeckodi, I have been waiting on this since 2003! I was supposed to attend university in September, and I had to defer my place with the hope that I would receive some good news between then and next August."

"To be honest, I did not believe that you had any leg to stand on, what with the fact that the last solicitor disposed of your passport in a box in Croydon. This is nothing but God!" professed Mrs. Jeckodi.

"Yes, it's God, nothing else!" I concurred.

"In two and a half years' time, you will need to reapply for another three years. You can come and I will represent you."

"Thank you so much, Mrs. Jeckodi. I will definitely contact you when I am approaching the deadline."

I signed some paperwork. I collected my documents, shook her hand, then floated out of her office.

Arriving at the salon, I confirmed that I got three years from the Home Office. Everyone congratulated me. I accepted the well wishes, then I proceeded to work for the rest of the day. The week went by like a weak scent of perfume—it was not memorable.

On Sunday, I started searching for retail jobs. I had a plan. I would secure a job where I could broaden my skill set, work a set time, and save some money towards my studies next September 2010. So, I commenced. After six weeks of searching, I got a bite. The third week of December, I heard from an assessment centre at a company's head office.

An extremely cold winter's morning, exiting Oxford Circus station was hazard prone. The heavens had opened, and the snowstorm was abnormal for the UK. Usually, it did not snow until late December or mid to late January. Fluffy snow poured from the sky, and it automatically made me happy. *This is a sign,* I thought.

Arriving at the head office was exciting. Kurt Geiger is viewed as a luxury brand and homegrown. The opportunity to work for this company made me extremely anxious, but I thought if I could use that feeling to fuel my enthusiasm, I would secure a role at the end of the assessment. After all, I loved shoes; my feet and legs were my best assets. I used to walk throughout the house in Jamaica in my mother's heels with the aspiration of representing Jamaica in Miss World or Miss Universe. Smiling, I shook my head in recollection. That was a pipe dream when I was twelve/thirteen because I did not grow one inch since my thirteenth birthday—five foot four then and now. But my constant remained true: my feet and legs were still my best assets, in my opinion.

The assessment kicked my ass. I was unlucky to grab the ugliest pair of shoes for the selling phase of the process. I believed that all my other phases were above average— yes, 100% self-praise and 100% naivety. On my way out of the building, I felt deflated. I had applied to this company four times, despite being rejected each time. I was doggedly focussed. If I did it then, I could do it again; I would simply dust myself off and find other companies to apply for. *I did my best. Whatever happens now, God, you take the wheel,* I proclaimed.

Two weeks passed and I heard nothing, so I kept applying to jobs. I wanted to leave the hair salon. I was tired of doing hair. The nostalgia had worn off and my body was always aching. And coming into immediate contact with fungus in customers' hair was causing my face to break out. I was over it.

One Wednesday afternoon, I received a phone call from the company enquiring whether I was still open to accept employment. With no hesitation, I said yes. They confirmed that a position was becoming available, but it would not be until February 2010. They asked me whether I would be open to the role—Retail Advisor—in February and after a couple of seconds, I said yes. They were happy and I was elated.

I felt that leaving the hair salon would be the best thing to do. Sandra was due to give birth any minute, so giving her ten weeks to find my replacement was the right thing to do, I contemplated. The next morning, I spoke to her privately. I delivered a verbal notice, and I confirmed that my last day would be the last Saturday in January.

The weeks that transpired afterwards were a living hell for me. Her friends would come into the salon and bully me both directly and indirectly. My workload doubled. I was deliberately isolated, and the cliques grew in dominance. Now, going to work gave me heartburns. Gradually, I started to lose appetite, then my weight fell off like succulent meat on bones. My trousers became baggy, and my collarbone became more pronounced. Bullying was a daily constant and to cope, I would mark off each day on my calendar every night after work.

The last Saturday of January, I kept my head down and stayed busy all day. At 10:00 p.m. that night, Sandra queried whether today was my last day.

I looked her square in the eye and said, "Yes. I start my new job on Monday, the first of February."

CHAPTER 10

BREAKTHROUGH

· · · · · · · · · · · · · · · · · · · ◆ · ◆ · · · · · · · · · · · · · · ·

Disembarking 345 bus in Camberwell Green, I was positively beaming. I was in the best shape of my life: size UK8, toned and my skin was glowing. Draped over my body was a luxurious black and grey, tie-dye cotton maxi-dress coupled with a pair of carved-out wooden wedges. *The heavens are surely smiling on me today,* I settled.

However, every time I caught other people's glances, I kept wondering who these people were staring at. My teenaged self, the one with chronic acne who struggled for five years to acquire normalcy, kept reminding me that . . . *it can't be you.* Yet sporadically, I felt like a million dollars.

The first guy that I fell in puppy love with, Alex Reid, had said to me, "I caught the prized fish!"

On this day, I truly felt like the prized fish. After migrating from Manchester, Jamaica, I never thought that I would see him again. Two months ago, the essence of him did not cross my mind. Memories of him were buried deep in my subconscious. Yet today, the pavement was my catwalk! The spotlight was on me. Walking towards him, I glanced at his familiar face. Six foot two and medium built, tanned olive skin, piercing eager eyes and a kind smile. Yep, there he was, my first official crush! I smiled to myself.

We hugged and walked into Crown to Sole to enquire about the possibility of booking him a massage and a facial. They had a position available within fifteen minutes. We were guided downstairs to the waiting area. Smiling with a little light flirting, people—especially the women who were also waiting—admired our display of affection towards each other.

"Alex Reid!" yelled a medium built and light-eyed lady; the masseuse.

Alex stood up and followed her. She looked in my direction and instructed me to follow her too. Entering the room, I immediately felt restricted by the confining space. It was a miniscule room that housed a massage bed and its complementary equipment. Alex was instructed to remove his shirt and mount the bed. In the process of receiving his facial, the masseuse made mention that we made a lovely couple. I was beaming because he was my childhood crush. The experience was seamless, and Alex was well in need of the pampering as he was a part-time cricketer who had been travelling.

The remainder of the day, I was Cinderella at the ball. He took me shopping down Oxford Street; we went for dinner and the rest of the week was like a whirlwind. He returned home that following weekend and promised to keep in touch. Weeks turned into months, and nothing, not a peep from him.

Filled with hurt and vengeance, I went hunting for him on the rocky streets of Facebook. Through sheer ingenuity, relentlessness, and tenacity, and jumping over a few hurdles, I found him.

He was "happily" married in the Bahamas with a son. I stumbled upon a picture of him with a lady and a young boy. They looked like a couple, and through my incessant determination, I learnt that the lady was his wife—Samantha—and the boy was his son. So, all those conversations where he was confidently addressing my name, he was able to do so because his "*wife*" had the same name as me. Inconsolable, my heart ached for weeks. I immersed all my focus into my new job and getting prepared to start my bachelors in September, building a protective shell around my heart..

HOW I FORCED PANDORA'S BOX SHUT

Hope Floats
***

Operating effectively at my new job took me through a steep learning curve. I was unaware that I struggled with speaking to strangers. Engaging in conversations with strangers was not the problem, it was more about my insecurity around my Jamaican accent and how it was interweaved with my temperamental British (South London) accent and dialect, which tended to happen when I was excited or passionate about a concept or an idea. Yes, feeling like an imposter was the unrelenting thorn that sat in my side and would not ease up.

My manager was cruel but kind. She had lashed out a few times, spewing emotionally insensitive statements and gestures. I had seen this page before, I would remind myself, so I kept my thoughts to myself and focussed on probing her for as much knowledge as I could. At the end of the day, she was one of the youngest managers in the company's history, so she must have been good!

After two years of employment at this establishment, I had been promoted to weekend supervisor at a standalone branch, which was different to the department store-based branches. I was now not only responsible for myself but the performance of a group of people. I worked all day Thursdays, Saturday, and Sundays, and the other days I would attend university and study into the early mornings of 3:00–4:00 a.m. Cognitively functioning and conducting myself took up the entire essence of my mental and physical fibre. Simply waking up each morning was a difficult task. Although extremely exhausted, I was operating above optimal, but had a 100% probability of imploding. I was exceptionally exhausted.

Visa Running Out!!
***

Two years and seven months had passed since the retrieval of my three-year visa. Effectively managing all my priorities were taking a toll on my physical and mental state. I had been running on empty for over two years.

On an early Friday morning, after weeks of scouring the internet seeking a legal aid solicitor, I discovered one. Even though I had promised Mrs. Jeckodi that I would contact her to reapply to the Home Office, her firm was in East London, and I lived on the other side of London, Southwest London, so travelling all that way was not convenient for me. At the discovery of my solicitor, my chest tightened as though I was experiencing an anxiety attack. Overwhelmingly nauseous, I dropped my head in between my legs. I breathed deeply and slowly to infiltrate my lungs with oxygen thus diminishing my dizziness. Hope pierced the darkness of my visa running out as I hurriedly dialled the solicitor's office.

Three rings later, a voice said, "Good morning, Balham Solicitors. Gabriella Newt speaking. How can I help?"

"Good morning, Gabriella. My name is Samantha White. I am seeking a solicitor who can help me to obtain indefinite leave to remain. I have three months left, and I would like to commence this application as soon as possible. Also, I am student, and I would like to know if any of the solicitors in your firm accept legal aid because I do not have much money."

"We have available a solicitor that has a free time slot at 2:00 p.m. today, who is an acceptor of legal aid clienteles. Is this convenient for you?"

"Yes, please; please schedule me for this appointment."

"You are booked in today for Mikal Joshua. See you this afternoon!"

"Should I bring anything?"

"Yes, bring your passport for now, and more will be discussed pertaining to what Mr. Joshua will require for you to commence your application."

"Thank you kindly, Ms. Newt. Thank you kindly indeed."

My emotions were barely contained, like they were in a satchel that was seeping through the seams. Hanging up the phone placed extra bolts around the perimeter.

"Phew!" *Thank you, Lord.*

"Balham Station!" sounded over the bus' speaker, piercing the silence that loomed lowly.

Exiting the bus, I was somewhat dubious and melancholy. I hated solicitors. This solicitor would be my fourth. *I hope it is the last,* I contemplated. I just wanted to be "**settled.**" I was sick and tired of this process. I had resided in the UK for almost ten years, and every second had drained me financially and emotionally. Thousands of dollars were being funnelled into the pockets of solicitors: good and bad. And unfortunately, my first two solicitors had sullied the water.

Now, I navigated the treacherous streets of "**the lawyers.**" The door of the solicitors' firm was white and unimpressionable. A plain white door with a simple unimaginative design stating "Balham Solicitors." Nervously bracing the door, I entered. On the right, I was greeted by a hopeful and kind smile.

"Good afternoon. Welcome to Balham Solicitors. How can I be of service to you?"

"Hi, good afternoon. My name is Samantha White. I have an appointment with a Mr. Joshua at 2:00 p.m."

"Aah, yes. Please have a seat and he will be with you in ten minutes," the receptionist replied while pointing to the seating area on the opposite side of her position.

Shortly after being seated in the waiting area, I was greeted by a tall, medium built, African man. Unsure about his integrity and moral compass, I returned a half-smile. I stood up for formalities, shook his hand and followed him through to his office.

"Mr. Joshua, I have encountered several unscrupulous solicitors that have done me wrong. To say that I am jaded is an understatement. After listening to my case, if you feel that you do not have the capabilities to effectively represent me, please let me know so that I can seek better representation."

"I understand that you have been scammed out of money on previous applications, and I sincerely apologise. When criminals muddy the waters, us good up-standing solicitors undergo a steep uphill climb to regain our clients' trust."

After the first consultation, my walls began to subside, and my trust in Mr. Joshua started to replenish in droplets.

Three months had passed, and my visa had completely run out. It was not a big deal because I had been here before, and according to the Home Office, if your application were sent off before your visa came to an end, you would remain in that state until you received a written outcome.

I was existing in my daily activities of school and work, as usual. One evening after school, I was blindsided by the discovery of a letter from my university requesting that I go to the Immigration Department in the registration office to provide my updated visa. Upon reading that sentence: ". . . your inability to provide the requested documents will result in negative consequences," my heart sank. *I am going to have to leave university?* This thought bounced around my head, swarming my thoughts like birds of prey. *I must finish university. I am the first in my family to attend, I must graduate.* I struggled to sleep all night. Dreams of being forced to leave university without a degree had me spiralling down throughout the night.

Entering the registration office, I felt sick, sick to my stomach at the thought of being so close to the end of completing my degree, but still so far away. I was approaching the end of my second year and functioning on pure adrenaline. Being turned away from my studies was a notion that I did not think that I could live with. I feared that this would be the final fracture that shattered my dome of aspiration.

After catching one of the officer's attention, I explained myself. "My documents are in the Home Office and based on its rules, I stay fixed in any situation until a decision is made by the Home Office."

"I will relay your information, and they will let you know," he said.

A week later, I further learnt that they rejected my explanation and requested that I leave my course. I immediately went to the registration office to speak to someone.

I saw the same gentleman that I had explained my situation to, and I asked him, "Is there anything that I can do?"

He advised me to get an official letter from my solicitor. I thanked him and left the office. Instantly, I rang Balham Solicitors and requested to speak with Mr. Joshua.

"Mr. Joshua, I need your advice and help."

CHAPTER 11

HOPE

"Yvonne, Yvonne, Yvonne !? Are you still coming tomorrow?" Probing her face for a response, I registered nothing. "So? Are you coming?"

I was starting to become quite agitated. She had been avoiding me, at this naming ceremony, all afternoon. I needed to know what her intentions were so that I could instruct her on where to meet me tomorrow because my friend was coming to pick me up and I needed to know where we could pick her up too.

"So? Can you please answer, so that I know how to plan my morning? Well!?" I insisted.

Yesterday, after finishing work as the supervisor of the retail store, I went to the hair salon where Yvonne worked.

I borrowed a razor to remove my weave. The weave had been installed by Yvonne the day before. I waited patiently for her to install my extensions all evening, but she stalled and dragged her feet. Then after she completed all her tasks, she commenced weaving my hair.

I had a tiny head—twenty-two inches in circumference—so if extensions were not evenly distributed over the area of my head, the result would always be underwhelming. This happened. My extensions were not installed to my expectations and having approximately five years' experience in the installation of extensions, I was extremely pedantic, particular and a perfectionist when it came to the presentation of my hair. And as it would be my graduation day on Monday, I needed my hair to be immaculate and timeless. Once I removed the extensions from my head, I went home.

Exhausted but determined, adrenaline coursed through my veins. The desire to have the perfect hairstyle for my graduation pictures consumed me and that kept me focussed all night.

As I looped the final thread through my extensions, the clock struck 7:00 a.m. It was Sunday morning. I was shattered. I collapsed into my bed which was framed by an explosion of rubbish—hair extension packages, rolls of thread, needles, clothes, and shoes.

Hope Overflows
***

"I am not coming."

My chest tightened. I was shocked. "What? You're not coming tomorrow?" I said in disbelief.

Stunned, I walked away in contemplation and regret. I was gutted. I could not believe Yvonne would do this to me. She had known me since I was fourteen years old. She had been by my side while navigating the trials that this life had thrown to me thus far: my mother being incarcerated, becoming homeless, experiencing being pimped out by her half-sister, and so much more. I considered her to be a mother figure. I looked up to her. I sought her advice and opinion at times of need. At this moment, which was extremely momentous to me, she was letting me down. To say that I was gutted was an understatement. Another person that I was depending on had let me down. I felt deflated.

Arriving home, I was determined to not let that dark cloud block my sun of achievement. I had sacrificed and worked so hard since the age of sixteen to get here. I would let nothing, and no one, rain on my parade. I ironed my dress. I laid it out along with my shoes on one side of my bed. Brushing off the negative emotions, I rang one of my closest friends, Punkie, to confirm what time she would be arriving at my house in the morning for us to attend my graduation together.

I was sombre. As I looked back on the challenges and disappointments that I had overcome over the years, tears gently streamed down my cheeks. *I did it!* I reflected. *I am almost there; I can taste it.*

"Punkie, please get to my house by 8:30 a.m. tomorrow morning!"

"Why so early?"

"We are travelling into Central London, and we must consider Monday morning traffic. We also need to ensure that I arrive at the venue on time to collect my gown and that you guys are seated."

"I am going out tonight."

"Why? When I asked you to attend my graduation, you made all these excuses. You had no babysitter for Khai, and now you are going out. I did not beg your mother to watch Khai so that you would go out. Can't you not go out this once, and stay overnight at mine so that we wake up and get ready together?"

"I can't. I have already made plans with Chum, Khai's dad."

"Just make sure that you don't stay out too long or have a hangover because you need to be at my house at 9:00 a.m."

"I will, definitely."

"Okay, if you say so. Just make sure that you are here on time tomorrow. See you then," I said dubiously.

Hanging up the phone, a negative feeling rose in me.

"She better turn up on time tomorrow," I moaned.

I had an early night. Tomorrow was the day. I wanted to be fresh-faced and well rested for my celebration—an emotional and physical representation that I had overcome the obstacles that were trying to block my path for the past nine years. *Did I force Pandora's box shut?* My thoughts lingered on that question as I dosed off.

"Where are you going?" asked a security guard.

"I am trying to get into the building," I said confusingly.

"Which building?" enquired the security guard.

"That building behind you," I said sternly while pointing at it.

"You can't enter; it's closed."

"What!? Why? How come? I need to hand in my dissertation!" Tears started to stream down my face. "If I don't hand it in, I will not pass or get the "***Honour***" included in my qualification," I pleaded with the security guard.

I started to cry inconsolably. The security guard could not calm me. I threw myself to the ground. The sound of my cry was piercing and forced everyone to stop and listen.

Suddenly, my eyes popped open. I felt dizzy. I searched around frantically trying to locate my phone. Once in my hand, the time said: 5:47 a.m., Monday. I collapsed back in bed to find my bearings. My head felt battered and bruised. With cracked lips, I craved water immensely.

I slowly got out of bed and headed to the kitchen where I located water and pain killers for my head. I then went back to bed for fifteen minutes, to help speed up the effects of the tablets that I consumed. Fifteen minutes later, I was up and was raring to go. While making breakfast, I started to call all my friends that I invited to decipher how far away they were.

Nothing. All the phone calls rang out to voicemails. *What is going on?* I questioned. I called non-stop for thirty minutes. Nothing. No answer. *Was my dream a foreshadowing of what would happen today?* As the clock struck 8:00 a.m., I started to panic. I commenced getting dressed. *No one would stand in my way or try to sabotage my day today. No one!* I promised.

As the hour hand struck 9:00 a.m., I was still waiting on my friends to arrive. Calmly, I placed my heels in a black carrier bag and forced my feet into my black leather pumps. I headed to the bus stop adjacent to my flat. Entering the tube station, I was a bag of nerves, and there was nobody by my side. I was able to contain my emotions on the underground with the armour of hope. I could not believe that everyone had let me down. My heart was on the floor, but this was my moment, and I could not let anything, or anyone, snatch it away from me.

Entering the graduation hall, I fell apart. I could not contain myself. Darting around the room, I saw a familiar face, Alicja, my classmate. Our friendship had grown over the past three years of our degree. She was Polish, and we were both Librans, so I had developed a great liking to her—she would say the things that I was thinking. Upon recognising that I was in tears, she came to my need, to be a shoulder to cry on. Once she cuddled me, I fell totally apart. Alicja consoled me for fifteen minutes. I literally cried my makeup off my face. We ventured to the bathroom to touch up our faces. While in the toilet, we heard the announcement of our degree.

"Sam, we need to go. It's time to line up!"

We squealed! In the blink of an eye, we were out the door. Alicja stood immediately in front of me as her surname was Weiz. We held each other's hands until it was her time to walk up and collect her certificate. Her parents and siblings (sister and brother) were in the audience cheering her on.

As for me, no one showed up. My mother got deported two years ago and my close friends had let me down. In a reflective state, I felt elated. I was proud of my determination and relentlessness to not give up on me when everyone else fell by the wayside. Whenever I desperately needed support from others, they always had let me down. Melancholy crept up on me and was trying to steal my day and my moment.

"Samantha White," said a voice, and it pierced through my thoughts, pulling me back to reality.

Aware of my location, I straightened up my gown and strolled across the platform. At one of the greatest moments of my life, I was experiencing it on my own. I panned across to the seats that I had purchased for my friends, and they were empty. I took my certificate and garnered positive energy deep down within me to plaster a smile upon my face. It was a smile that represented accomplishment and relief.

I had fought a good fight. I reluctantly took on all the curses that were released in my direction due to the negligence of my mother. I did it. I made it. I fought a good fight.

ABOUT THE AUTHOR

After completing a three month long holistic cleansing—including a vegan diet, emotional and spiritual cleansing—a crystal-clear vision came to me one night. It was the beginnings of this book, an account of my struggles and challenges that were never in vain, for I genuinely believe I went through them to someday inspire others.

I am a strong advocate of the school of thought that God and the universe join forces through alignment only when requested to bring one's purpose to life. God promises that he will establish us at the area of our greatest affliction. Through the thorn that remains unmoved, our purpose is revealed. This book is connected to my purpose, and my thorn is my journey as an immigrant teenager. Although discarded on the difficult streets of London, I was daring and determined to survive.

I recently obtained a master's degree in Business with Consulting from Warwick University. I continue to work on overcoming my fears while I remain committed to achieving my purpose.

You can reach me on social media at:
Facebook -
/samantha.whickeisha

Instagram -
samantha_white_author

Twitter - @Samanth41788140

Printed in Great Britain
by Amazon

10831112R10088